COMPU !

The ultimate s a professional, competent, honest, considerate, on-time, fairly-priced and dependable computer consultant

Read this book and you'll discover:

- ✓ The five types of technical support available, and the pros and cons of each.
- ✓ 5 critical facts you must know before moving to the cloud.
- ✓ How to avoid getting ripped off, disappointed and/or paying for substandard work.
- ✓ 12 warning signs that you hired the wrong computer consultant.
- ✓ Viruses, worms, spyware and hackers: what you need to know to protect your company from a cyber invasion.
- ✓ Everything you need to know about contracts, payment schedules and rate negotiations.
- ✓ 21 revealing questions you should ask any computer consultant before giving them access to your company's network.
- ✓ Why you need to avoid "cheap" or "bargain" computer repair shops.
- ✓ How to turn technology into a competitive advantage instead of a drain on your time, money and resources.
- ✓ Why your business needs managed services.

Master Technology Strategist for Business:

Greg Hanna

Co-author of *COMPUTERS SHOULD JUST WORK*, the Only Business Owner's Guide for Finding a Professional, Competent, Honest, Considerate, On-Time, Fairly-Priced and Dependable Computer Consultant

Greg Hanna
TOSS C3
153 Northboro Road
Southborough, MA, 01772
888-884-8677 • 508-820-2990
www.tossc3.com

Helping Business Owners Eliminate
Technology Headaches Finally and Forever

First Printing: 2016

ISBN 978-1-4951-9019-3

TOSS C3 Publishing
153 Northboro Rd, Suite 21
Southborough, MA 01772

www.TOSS.com

Dedication

This book is dedicated to the TOSS C3 staff, who say what I don't know could fill a book. They were right. Here's the book.

Table of Contents

Foreword

This book by Greg Hanna provides invaluable advice on choosing the right consultant before you hand over the keys to your castle.

Greg has had an extensive and successful career in Information Technology, spanning from System Automation of the 80's to Personalization of Business in the 90's and the latest sensation known as The Cloud. His years of experience provides Greg with a deep understanding of the ins and outs of best-practices when choosing the best technology direction for your company.

This book explains everything from the types of technical support available, characteristics to look at and the best questions to ask when trying to determine if the cloud is right for you. The nine chapters include The Downside of Technology, Avoiding Project Nightmares, Moving to the Cloud, How to Get the Most out of Your Computer Consultant and much more.

"Computers Should Just Work!" will prove to be a valuable resource to Business Owners, Firm Administrators, IT Managers and anyone hoping to guide their company down the right path with technology choices.

We look forward to hearing your great stories as you successfully navigate your way to the Cloud!

Mike Ciulla
Operations Manager
TOSS Corporation

Introduction

Business Is Becoming (Technically) More Complicated

There is a powerful force driving all businesses to deliver superior products and services faster and on tighter margins—technology.

Every business, from small mom-and-pop shops to large enterprises, is developing a strong reliance on technology. Whether it is e-mail, e-commerce, websites, cloud computing, database management or accounting software, or other line of business applications, there are very few businesses that don't have some level of dependency on their computer network and the various applications and data it stores.

The upside of technological advances is tremendous. When applied correctly, technology can provide your business significant competitive advantages in speed to market, increased productivity, improved customer service, and up-to-the-minute reporting for strategic planning and decision making.

Downside Of Technology

The downside of this vast dependency on technology is that, when it doesn't work, it can become a tremendous source of frustration, putting a major strain on your company's production, customer relations, sales and fulfillment. No business is immune from computer problems and failures. Without proper maintenance, the average business can end up with spyware, viruses and system crashes that can easily turn into major network outages. Not to mention the daily computer "glitches" and problems that already are frustrating you and your employees.

Let's talk about computer system complexity. Installing and supporting even a small network requires specialized knowledge and skills that most business owners don't have in-house, and the margin for error is greatly reduced in a small business. If a large corporation makes a $50,000 technology mistake, it's certainly not a good thing, but it only represents a minor blip in their overall IT budget. If a small business makes a $20,000, or even a $10,000, technology mistake, it could significantly impact their cash flow and potentially, their profitability!

If you're like most business owners, you probably shy away from things technical in nature because you don't understand how they work, why they work, or how to operate them. After all, what you want are business solutions that drive sales and profitability, not whiz-bang gadgets and budget-busting non-solutions that break and make your life more complicated. Yet the technology that runs your business is too important and too expensive to ignore.

- ✓ So how do you make sure that the hardware, software and systems you are investing in actually support your business goals and will work the way they are supposed to?
- ✓ How do you stay on top of technological advances that will give you significant competitive advantages while steering clear of the "latest and greatest" techno-fads?
- ✓ How do you make sure your data is protected from an ever-growing list of cyber-threats, including viruses, hackers, spyware, faulty hardware and software, and even employee sabotage?
- ✓ And ultimately, how do you go about finding a reliable consultant who not only has the expertise to make all of this technology work for you, but also the business acumen to recommend and implement

real solutions that enhance productivity and profitability?

That's what this book is about: arming you with the basic information you need to find a trusted advisor who can help your business tame technology and turn it into a powerful, competitive weapon instead of a huge financial strain and source of problems.

Computer Consultant Horror Stories

Unfortunately, there is no shortage of horror stories about unbelievably bad customer service from technology companies and computer consultants. They range from annoying computer support technicians who take forever to return a phone call to horror stories about fly-by-night computer repair shops or consultants who delete all the data stored on a network as a result of their unethical or incompetent behavior. If you talk with your own friends and colleagues, I'm sure you'll get an earful of the unfortunate experiences they have encountered in this area.

The biggest reason for this is that the computer services industry is not regulated like many other industries. Almost anyone who can turn on a computer can set up a computer repair shop, regardless of their actual knowledge and expertise. Compare this to electricians, plumbers, lawyers, realtors, dentists, doctors and accountants (to name a few) who are heavily regulated to protect the consumer from receiving substandard work or getting ripped off. However, because the computer industry is still relatively new, there aren't many laws in existence to protect the consumer.

The upside is that most computer consultants are ethical and will not try to cheat you or take advantage of you. But unethical computer consultants aren't the biggest problem—*incompetent* consultants are. Even if they are honestly trying to do a good job, their inexperience can cost you dearly in inflated support bills, poor network performance, weak cyber-security and data loss.

That is where this book will come in handy. It gives you basic, need-to-know facts to help you find an honest, competent consultant who can contribute to your business' success. By arming more business owners with this information, I am hoping to raise the standards within the computer repair and support industry, and to give you, the consumer, information to help you guard against the unethical conduct or incompetence of some companies and consultants.

Note: While there are plenty of women in the computer consulting industry, the large majority are men. For simplicity, I will therefore refer to computer consultants in the masculine gender throughout this book. You will also notice that I sometimes use the term "computer consultant," and sometimes the word "technician." Both refer to the person providing advice, products, services and support for your computer network. However, "consultant" is used to define someone with a higher level of expertise and knowledge, whereas "technician" connotes someone who simply knows how to fix computers.

What This Book Will Teach You

- How to become an educated buyer of IT support and services and avoid getting ripped off.
- How to reduce your IT costs.
- How to secure your network and data from viruses, spyware, hackers, corruption, loss, natural disasters, and disgruntled employees.
- How to eliminate computer problems and headaches that frustrate you and waste your time.
- How to turn technology into a competitive advantage instead of a drain on your time, money, and resources.

Chapter One

Bad Advice, Faulty Repairs & Incompetence

Every business, large or small, depends on technology at some level to operate. If you've owned a computer for more than five minutes, you know that no one is exempt from computer problems, system crashes and downtime. While all business owners can relate to the sheer frustration these issues create, few can put a dollar figure to the actual hard cost to their business. That is because so much of it is soft costs related to productivity, hours worked and time lost.

What makes the cost of computer downtime even more difficult to determine is the fact that no business is "average," and therefore statistics that quantify the cost of downtime for the average company are inaccurate.

However, no business owner can deny that an interruption in their business costs them money, whether that interruption is caused by a server crash, hardware failure or some other outside force. If you've ever had your business grind to a screeching halt because you and your employees could not access the data or systems necessary for operations, you must have some idea of the frustration and financial loss to your business, even if you didn't put a pencil to figuring out the exact cost.

Take a look at these statistics:

- Companies experience an average of 501 hours of network downtime every year, and the overall downtime costs an average of 3.6% of annual revenue. *(Source: The Costs of Enterprise Downtime, Infonetics Research)*
- 93% of companies that lost their data center for 10 days or more due to a disaster, filed for bankruptcy within one

year of the disaster, and 50% filed for bankruptcy immediately. *(Source: National Archives & Records Administration in Washington)*

- 20% of small to medium businesses will suffer a major disaster causing loss of critical data every 5 years. *(Source: Richmond House Group)*
- Last year, 40% of small to medium businesses that manage their own network and use the Internet for more than e-mail had their network accessed by a hacker, and more than 50% didn't even know they were attacked. *(Source: Gartner Group)*
- Of those companies participating in the Contingency Planning & Management Cost of Downtime Survey, 46% said each hour of downtime would cost their companies up to $50,000; 28% said each hour would cost between $51,000 and $250,000; 18% said each hour would cost between $251,000 and $1 million; and 8% said it would cost their companies more than $1 million per hour. *(Source: Cost of Downtime Survey Results, 2001)*
- Cybercriminals stole an average of $900 from each of 3 million Americans in the past year, and that doesn't include the hundreds of thousands of PCs rendered useless by spyware. *(Source: Gartner Group)*

But even if you don't factor in the soft costs of lost productivity, there is the hard cost of repairing and restoring your network. Most major network repairs will require an average of 4-8 hours to get the network back up and running. Plus, most consultants can't get on-site to resolve the problem for 24 to 48 hours. That means your network could be down for one to two days.

Since the computer consultants usually charge over $100 per hour, plus a trip fee and a surcharge if it's an emergency, the average cost of these repairs for a small network is $600-$1,000.

Over the course of a year, this results in $1,800-$3,000 in costs, not including hardware and software or lost sales and work hours. Naturally, those numbers will quickly multiply with larger, more complex networks.

The Cost of Bad Advice

In addition to downtime, there is another expense that most business owners don't consider: the cost of bad advice when an inexperienced consultant recommends a product, service or project that is unnecessary or incorrect for your specific situation.

Another form of bad advice is when a computer consultant doesn't take into consideration all the pitfalls and situations that will arise when implementing your project, and grossly underestimates the time and money it will take to successfully complete it. When a consultant makes this mistake, your project ends up way over schedule and over budget, costing you 2-3 times as much in unexpected fees, hardware and software.

It's gotten so bad that *Network World* recently noted, "Increasingly, IT customers are crying malpractice and railing against slipped implementation schedules, compounded consulting fees, and disappointing product performance."

Although the price of bad advice is hard to measure, if you've ever been disappointed or burned by an "IT expert," you know the costs to your business are painfully high.

Here are just a few of the ways bad IT advice can cost you:

- Paying for unnecessary projects, software or hardware.
- Paying too much for repairs, software and hardware.
- Accumulating downtime, unstable networks, data loss and security breaches.

- Getting stuck with a "solution" that doesn't really solve your problems.
- Increasing the time and work you and your employees invest in rolling out a project.
- Paying double by having a competent consultant fix what the first person messed up or complete the project you originally wanted implemented.
- Incurring litigation costs to get your money back from a technician who ripped you off.
- Dealing with the sheer frustration of the problems resulting from poor advice.

Trouble is, it's hard to know that you're paying for bad advice until you are already neck-deep into the problems. By the time you get the first inkling that you hired the wrong person, you've already invested a considerable amount of time and money, making it difficult, if not impossible, to end the project and look for someone else. That's why the information in this book is so critical. Your best defense against all this heartache is to become an educated consumer who does your homework.

Chapter Two

What Are Your Options for Technical Support?

With the constant changes to technology and the daily development of new threats, even a small network requires ongoing maintenance from a highly-trained consultant to ward off viruses, spam, spyware, slowness, user errors and data loss. However, hiring a full-time IT person is not always feasible for small to medium sized businesses. If your business can't justify hiring an IT manager, you only have three options for computer support:

Option #1: Don't do anything.

This is really foolish, but we see it every day: businesses that don't pay attention to the care and maintenance of their network until it stops working. Then they are forced to call in an expert to repair or replace whatever caused the problem.

This reactive model of network support is similar to ignoring oil and filter changes in your car until smoke starts pouring out from under the hood. Taking a reactive approach to network maintenance is a surefire path to extensive downtime, lost data and excessive spending on IT support, not to mention major disruptions in staff productivity, sales, production and customer service. Even if your computer network appears to be working fine, there are a number of daily, weekly and monthly maintenance tasks that must be performed to keep your data secure and your system running smoothly. A short list of these tasks includes:

- Virus scans and updates
- Security patches and updates
- System backups and disaster-recovery planning and testing

- Spyware detection and removal
- Server and desktop optimization
- Employee policies and monitoring
- Intrusion detection
- Spam filtering

If you run specialized practice-management, customer-relationship management, or production software, or if you have multiple locations, a wireless network, highly sensitive data (as in financial or medical organizations), or other specialized needs, the list will get longer. Remember, your computer network is just like your car or your house. They all need regular proactive maintenance to avoid problems.

If you learn only one lesson from this book, I hope it will be to proactively monitor, maintain and secure your network instead of choosing to react to network and computer problems as they arise. Aside from a telephone, your computer network and the data on it are undoubtedly the most important business tools in your office. When they are unavailable, all productive work comes to a grinding halt.

As the old saying goes, an ounce of prevention is worth a pound of cure; this goes double for your computer network. Unfortunately, most business owners are under the incorrect assumption that regular computer maintenance is not necessary, and therefore only call in an experienced consultant when something goes wrong. As we stated previously, this model of "break-fix" computer support is not a good idea, especially if the operation of your network and the data on it are important to your business.

Option #2: Do it yourself.

Although this option is better than doing nothing, it still puts you at risk for computer network disasters. Instead of hiring a qualified consultant to support your network, you designate the most technically-knowledgeable person on staff to be your makeshift IT manager, and bring in outside help only when you run into a network crisis you can't solve.

Problem is, you are pulling these people away from the real job you hired them to do, and unless they have the time to stay up-to-date on the latest developments in IT support, security and management, they don't have the skills or time required to properly maintain and secure your network and could actually worsen the situation. This inevitably results in a network that is ill-maintained and unstable, which may cause excessive downtime, overspending on IT support, and expensive recovery costs.

Another variation of this option is to get your neighbor's kid or a friend to provide computer support on a part-time basis. This is a mistake for two reasons: First, they may not be fully qualified to handle the job, so they could make things worse. They may be able to fix the problem in the short-term, but they might not have the time or expertise to get to the root of the matter. Second, they may not always be available when you need them. If your server goes down at 9:00 AM, they might not be able to come until later that day or evening, or next week, causing you to lose a full day or more of productivity.

Also, as mentioned previously, they are providing reactive support. As with all things in life and business, it is far less expensive to prevent problems than to clean them up. If your part-time technician is not performing regular maintenance and monitoring of your network, you are susceptible to more problems.

Option #3: Outsource your support to a competent consultant.

Obviously, this is going to be the fastest and surest way to solve your computer problems. However, there are an ever-growing number of companies springing up across the country that offer computer repair services and support, which makes it difficult for a business owner to know which vendor is right for them.

As it stands today, there are five types of external computer support you can use:

1. **Vendor support:**

   Phone support provided by Dell, HP, Microsoft, or any of the big software and hardware vendors. If you've ever tried to get technical support from a large manufacturer or store, you know how frustrating it can be.

   First, many vendors don't provide free support. If they do, it is usually very limited and only available by e-mail or Web response forms. If you are lucky enough to reach the support department, you'll end up going through a maze of phone options before you get a live person, and then the person is usually a nontechnical customer service representative who can't provide any real assistance. In most cases, they'll be located in another country, and may even be difficult to understand (many technology companies outsource their customer service because it's cheaper than employing U.S. workers). You'll also get a different person every time you call, and most will not have any particular knowledge about your business or what you are trying to achieve.

   Here's another problem with vendor support: They aren't going to help you solve problems that aren't related directly to their hardware or software. For example, let's suppose you're having trouble connecting to the Internet, so you call your local provider. If their service is not causing the problem, you're stuck. Maybe your firewall is not configured correctly. Maybe the cable is not connected properly. If your problem is even partially related to another software or piece of hardware on your system, they won't help you.

2. **Computer support hotline services:**

These services work like prepaid calling cards. For a set fee, you'll get an 800 number to call for 24-7 technical support. Sounds reasonable, but it's not all it's cracked up to be.

If you are a home user with simple application problems and questions, this service may work well for you. However, if you are a business with mission-critical data, the last thing you want is a junior technician giving you advice. Also, some problems simply need to be analyzed on-site. Finally, these services are set up to deliver basic computer support, not to troubleshoot server problems, help with data recovery, or provide proactive maintenance.

3. **The part-time technician just getting started:**

This is usually someone who left a job in the IT department of a company, got fired, or lost a job due to downsizing. Either way, he decided to start his own business with the dream of making lots of money by providing computer support to small businesses.

In many cases, he will try to do a good job for you. He means well, will often work cheap, and is usually eager to please. He might even have been referred to you by a friend or business colleague.

Although he has every intention of providing you with a good service, there are some things you need to consider before hiring him to work on your network. Since most of these folks work from home, they don't have a secretary or office staff to handle your requests. When you call, you'll either get:

- An answering machine.
- A spouse, friend or child who will take a message (which might or might not reach the technician).
- No answer and no voice mail; the phone just keeps ringing.
- The technician on his cell phone. Unfortunately, he's usually at another client's site, in his car, or taking care of some personal business (you catch him at the doctor's office or in a noisy restaurant).

The problem with this choice is response time; if you have a major network crisis, you need to know that you can get in touch with your consultant AND get a call back or response immediately. But it doesn't end there …

Another problem you'll encounter is availability; the technician might not always be around when you need him. What happens if he leaves town for a week or has to go to the hospital? Or two or more of his clients experience a major emergency at the same time? Or the going gets tough and he decides to take another job? These are all scenarios that happen frequently with computer technicians who haven't established best practices and systems in their businesses. And if he is only supporting your network part-time, you can bet your emergency is going to take a back seat to his full-time employer.

Guaranteeing his work is another problem for the part-timer. Most don't have a professional contract, proposal or invoice to give you, which means you have no written paperwork or contractual agreements to fall back on if things go wrong. Plus, most don't carry insurance, and can't compensate you if they accidentally screw up your network or cause you to lose data.

Even if he guarantees his work, how do you know he'll be around to fulfill his promises? Addresses and phone numbers can be changed instantly, and your one-man-wonder can disappear, leaving you no recourse or recovery.

4. The "major player" tech-support company:

This vendor is the complete opposite of the one-man-band. They may have multiple technicians, multiple locations and a support crew. They might even have locations across the globe. There are many first-rate computer-support companies in this category that can be trusted to do a good job for you. As a matter of fact, many have the staff and resources to do an outstanding job.

So what's the problem? Their schedule, price, relevant technology, availability! In many cases, these companies are so busy servicing a number of large, profitable clients that they might not give a small to medium business owner the service, response time and support you want. These companies are deeply entrenched in "box moving" technologies and in most cases do not recommend or even offer modern methods of IT delivery best suited for the small and mid-sized businesses, such as flat fee IT or completely hosted IT on a pay per person basis. They also may charge you exorbitant fees to cover their massive overhead of staff and offices. If you own a big business, with a big IT budget, you'll do just fine with this type of company. However, if you own a small or medium business with a conservative IT budget, this may not be the best option for you.

Since you don't represent a large windfall of profits for them, big tech-support companies may delegate their junior technicians, who are just learning the ropes, to support your network, saving the experienced consultants for their more profitable clients. As a business owner yourself, you can hardly blame them for taking this approach but, as a customer, you don't want to be the small fish who is easily brushed aside.

Just like the big vendors, the larger the tech-support companies get, the less personalized the service becomes. You may not always get the same consultant working on your network, and you might not be able to talk directly with a consultant when you call. Being part of a large franchise doesn't guarantee great service either; it just means they were able to write a check to cover the franchise costs. That doesn't automatically buy them good business sense, technical skills and/or customer-focused service.

5. **A privately-owned Information Technology firm that provides an Enterprise experience to the small and medium sized business segment:**

You might accuse me of being biased here, but please give me a minute to explain my position before you dismiss my advice.

First of all, I've been doing business in this industry for 30 years, so I have considerable experience working with, and talking to, hundreds and hundreds of computer consultancy's of all sizes. I've seen the horror stories and heard the complaints business owners and executives have with all technology service vendors. The business you choose to support your network should be large enough to provide back-up support and fast response times, but small enough to provide personal service. That is the way we've modeled our company, and we've been able to deliver consistent, professional services.

We certainly don't feel as though our model is the sole option you can choose, and the size of a company is certainly not the only way to know in advance how professional and competent they will be. There are firms in all the choices outlined above that will do a great job for you.

The remainder of this book will further outline what to look for when choosing a computer consultant for your business.

Chapter Three

Secrets to Choosing a Great Computer Consultant

Choosing a computer support company isn't easy. There are no shortages of horror stories about incompetent computer repair "gurus" bungling jobs and causing MORE problems as a result of their loose morals or gross incompetence. I'm sure if you talk to your own friends and colleagues you will get an ear-full of the unfortunate experiences they have encountered in this area.

Why is this? Because the computer repair and consulting industry, along with a lot of other industries, has its own share of incompetent or unethical businesses who will try to take advantage of trusting business owners who simply do not have the ability to determine whether or not they know what they are doing. Sometimes this is out of greed for your money; but more often it's simply because they don't have the skills and competency to do the job right, but won't tell you that up front. From misleading information, unqualified technicians, poor management and terrible customer service, we've seen it all…and we know they exist in abundance because we have had a number of customers come to us to clean up the disasters they have caused.

Buyer Beware: The Computer Repair And Consulting Industry Is NOT Regulated

Here's an embarrassing (and little-known) fact about my industry: it is not regulated like many other professional service industries which means ANYONE can claim they are a "computer repair expert." In fact, a lot of the businesses in this industry started because the owner was FIRED or laid off from their job and couldn't find work anywhere else. That means many of the so-called experts are useless and make the sleazy auto repair shops look like the pinnacle of virtue and competence.

Electricians, plumbers, insurance, lawyers, realtors, dentists, doctors, accountants, etc. are heavily regulated to protect the consumer from receiving substandard work or getting ripped off. However, the computer industry is still highly unregulated and there aren't any laws in existence to protect the consumer – which is why it's so important for you to arm yourself with the information contained in this report.

Anyone who can hang out a shingle can promote themselves as a computer expert. Even if they are honestly trying to do a good job for you, their inexperience can cost you dearly in your network's speed and performance or in lost or corrupt data files.

The 4 Most Costly Misconceptions about Computer Maintenance and Repair

Misconception #1: My computer network doesn't need regular monitoring and maintenance.

This is probably one of the biggest and most costly misconceptions that business owners have. Usually this is because they've been fortunate enough to never have encountered a major disaster; but that's similar to someone thinking they don't need to wear a seat belt when driving a car because they've never had an accident.

Computer networks are complex and dynamic systems that need regular updates and maintenance to stay up, running fast and problem free. In fact, it's surprising how fast a brand-new PC will slow down after a few weeks of use without proper updates and maintenance. Here are just a FEW of the critical updates that need to be done on a weekly – if not daily – basis:

- Security patches applied – with NEW viruses and hacker attacks cropping up DAILY, this is a CRITICAL part of maintaining your network
- Antivirus updates and monitoring
- Firewall updates and monitoring
- Backup monitoring and test restores
- Disaster recovery testing and adjustments
- Spam filter installation and updates
- Spyware detection and removal
- Monitoring disk space on workstations and servers
- Monitoring hardware for signs of failure
- Optimizing systems for maximum speed
- Monitoring for rogue application memory leaks

Just like a car, if you don't change the oil, replace the filter, rotate the tires, flush the transmission, and perform other regular maintenance on your car, it will eventually break down and cost you FAR MORE to repair than the cost of the basic maintenance – and cars are far simpler than a computer network!

If your computer support tech does not insist on some type of regular, automated monitoring or maintenance of your network, then DO NOT HIRE THEM. Lack of system maintenance is the NUMBER ONE reason most people end up losing valuable files and incurring heavy computer repair bills. If your technician isn't offering you these services, you need to find someone else to support your computer or network for two reasons:

1. Either they don't know enough to make this recommendation or don't have a proactive monitoring system in place. Either is a sure sign they are horribly inexperienced, *OR*

2. They recognize that they are ***profiting*** from your computer problems and don't want to recommend steps towards preventing you from needing their help on an ongoing basis. After all, they'll get paid MORE to remove a virus than to make sure your system is patched, updated and secured (which can be done quickly and inexpensively with good monitoring).

Either reason is a good one to get as far away from that company as possible! The fact is, there are so many metrics that need to be constantly monitored per device, to ensure a smooth working system, a human-being is just not capable of doing the work without the aid of a finally tuned automated proactive monitoring system.

Misconception #2: My nephew/neighbor's kid/brother-in-law/office manager knows this computer stuff and can take care of our computers.

Most people look for a part time "guru" for one reason: to save a few bucks; but this often comes back to haunt them. We frequently get calls from business owners who desperately need our help to get them back up and running or to clean up a mess that was caused by an inexperienced neighbor, friend, or relative who was just trying to help.

If the person you have working on your machine does not do computer repair and support for a living, there is a good chance they won't have the knowledge or experience to truly help you – they are a hobbyist at best. And do you really want a part-time, inexperienced person responsible for handling something as important as your data and computer network? As with everything in life, you get what you pay for. That's not to say you need to go broke to find a great technician, but you shouldn't be choosing someone on price alone.

Misconception #3: All computer technicians are created equal. Your best option will be the one who offers the lowest price.

As we stated a moment ago, you get what you pay for. A cheap price usually means a cheap job. Really good technicians do NOT work cheap because they are in high demand just like every other professional service category. The only technicians that will work cheap are those that are just starting and they are grossly inexperienced.

And some shops will hire college kids or newbie technicians because they will work for next to nothing to gain experience, OR they allow interns to support your network because they don't have to pay them at all – but what you don't realize is than an inexperienced technician like this can end up costing more because:

1. They improperly diagnose problems, which mean you're paying them to fix the WRONG thing and STILL won't resolve your problem. Case in point: A few years ago a TV reporter went undercover to 8 computer repair shops in LA with a perfectly working PC, but simply disconnected a cable on the system board (a fix that the AVERAGE computer tech would have caught in minutes with a visual inspection). Several shops improperly diagnosed the problem and wanted to charge them anywhere from $59 to over $275 to fix it!

2. They could take 3 to 5 times as long to do the same repair an experienced technician could fix quickly. Again, you're paying for those extra hours.

3. They could do MORE damage, costing you more money and downtime.

With your client data, accounting records, e-mail and other critical data at stake, do you REALLY want the lowest-priced shop working on your machine?

We take the view that most people want value for money and simply want the job done right. In my own business, I decided a long time ago that I would rather explain our higher rates ONE TIME than to make excuses for POOR SERVICE forever.

Misconception #4: An honest computer support company should be able to give you a quote over the phone.

I wish this were true, but it isn't. Just like a good doctor, an honest and professional technician will need to diagnose your network before they can quote any price over the phone; consider the example above where all was needed was a simple cable being plugged in. If someone brought that to us, we would just plug it back in and not charge them; but without SEEING the machine, we could have never diagnosed that over the phone.

Also, some consultants will quote you a cheap rate over the phone to get in the door, but then jack up the prices once they get in your office by taking 3 times as long, selling you add-ons and up-grades, etc. And finally, reputable firms don't charge by the hour anyway -- they give you a fixed, flat rate. Here's why…

One of the easiest ways to take advantage of a customer is to get them to agree to a time and materials repair. Unless you know what's wrong and how long it should take, they can soak you on the fees. And what are you going to do when they get 5-6 hours into a repair or project and then spring on you the news that it will take even longer than they anticipated to fix, costing you MORE money?

Always, always, always make sure you get a flat-rate, fixed fee quote in advance so you don't end up getting burned – and NEVER take a phone quote!

21 Questions You Should Ask Your Computer Consultant Before Hiring Them To Support Your Network

Customer Service:

Q1: Do they answer their phones live or do you always have to leave a voice mail and wait for someone to call you back?

Any reputable computer consultant will answer their phones live from at least 8:00 am to 5:00 pm and give all clients an emergency after hours number they may call if a problem arises, including weekends. Why? Because many CEOs and executives work outside normal hours and find it to be the most productive time they have. If they cannot access their computer network AND can't get hold of anyone to help them, it's incredibly frustrating.

Q2: Do they have a written, guaranteed response time to your calls?

Your computer consultant must guarantee to have a technician working on your problem within a certain timeframe after you call. If they can't guarantee a certain response time, then be prepared to work on their timeframe and not yours when a problem does arise. A written guaranteed response time should be standard in every service agreement you sign.

Q3: Do they take the time to explain what they are doing and answer your questions in terms that you can understand (not geek-speak), or do they come across arrogant and make you feel stupid for asking simple questions?

Good technicians are trained to have the 'heart of a teacher' and will take time to answer your questions and explain everything in simple terms.

Q4: Do they consistently (and proactively) offer new ways to improve your network's performance, or do they wait until you have a problem to make recommendations?

Your computer consultant should routinely conduct quarterly review meetings with you to look for new ways to help improve their operations, lower costs, increase efficiencies and resolve any problems that may be arising. Their goal should be to help you be more profitable, efficient and competitive.

Q5: Do they provide detailed invoices that clearly explain what you are paying for?

Do you hate it when your computer service company sends you a bill and you have no idea what work was done? This is completely unacceptable behavior. You should demand that your computer consultant provide you with detailed invoices that show what work was done, why and when so you never have to guess what you are paying for.

Q6: Do they have adequate cyber-liability, errors and omissions insurance, and workers compensation insurance to protect YOU?

Here's something to consider: if THEY cause a problem with your network that causes you to be down for hours or days or to lose data, who's responsible? Here's another question to consider: if one of their technicians gets hurt at your office, who's paying? In this litigious society we live in, you better make sure whomever you hire is adequately insured at a minimum with both errors and omissions insurance AND workers compensation. In today's world, I would insist that they have adequate cyber-liability insurance, and suggest that your company consider a cyber policy as well.

True Story: A few years ago Geek Squad was slapped with multi-million dollar lawsuits from customers for bad behavior of their technicians. In some cases, their techs where accessing, copying and distributing personal information they gained access to on customers PCs and laptops brought in for repairs. In other cases they lost a client's laptop (and subsequently all the data on it) and tried to cover it up. Bottom line, make sure the company you are hiring has proper insurance to protect YOU.

Q7: Do they guarantee to complete projects on time and on budget?

All projects should be a fixed priced and guaranteed to be completed on time, in writing. This is important because many unethical or incompetent computer guys will only quote "time and materials," which gives them free reign to nickel and dime you as well as take as much time as needed on completing a project.

Maintenance of Your Network:

Q8: Do they insist on remotely monitoring your network 24/7/356 to keep critical security settings, virus definitions and security patches up-to-date and PREVENT problems from turning into downtime, viruses, lost data and other issues?

A remote network monitoring system watches over your network to constantly look for developing problems, security issues and other problems so your computer consultant can address them BEFORE they turn into bigger problems and network downtime.

Q9: Do they provide you with a regular report that shows all the updates, security patches, and status of every machine on your network so you know for SURE your systems have been secured and updated?

Request a detailed report that shows an overall health score of your network and the updates to your antivirus, security settings, patches and other important network checks (like hard drive space, backups, speed and performance, etc.). Even if you don't read through the report, it's important to know that this is happening.

Q10: Is it standard procedure for them to provide you with written, network documentation detailing what software licenses you own, critical passwords, user information, hardware inventory, etc., or are they the only person with the "keys to the kingdom?"

Every business should have this in written and electronic form at no additional cost.

Side Note: You should NEVER allow an IT person to have that much control over you and your company. If you get the suspicion that your current IT person is keeping this under their control as a means of job security, fire them. This is unethical and dangerous to your organization, and should not be tolerated.

Q11: Do they have other technicians on staff who are familiar with your network in case your regular technician goes on vacation or gets sick?

Since they are keeping detailed network documentation and updates on your account, any of their technicians should be able to pick up where another one has left off.

Q12: When they offer an "all-inclusive" support plan, is it TRULY all-inclusive, or are their "gotchas" hidden in the fine print?

One of the more popular service plans offered by consulting firms today is an "all-inclusive" managed services plan. These are actually a good thing because they'll save you a lot of money in the long run – HOWEVER, make sure you REALLY understand what is and isn't included. Some things to consider are:

- Is phone/e-mail help desk included, or extra?
- What about network upgrades, moves, or user changes?
- Is hardware and/or software included?
- What about 3rd party software support? (We recommend that this IS included).
- What are the costs/consequences of early cancellation?
- What if you aren't happy with their services? Do they offer a money-back guarantee?
- If the hardware and software is included, what happens if you cancel the contract?
- Is offsite backups included? To what degree?
- If you have a major disaster, is restoring your network included or extra?
- What about onsite support calls or remote office support?

Backups and Disaster Recovery:

Q13: Do they INSIST on monitoring an offsite as well as an onsite backup, or are they letting you rely on outdated tape backups?

I would never allow any business these days to use tape backups because they are incredibly unreliable. You should implement an appliance based solution which uses Cloud on Write® technology. This will allow immediate local recovery, your data is securely offsite, and enable you to run your business remotely, should your physical office suffer a catastrophe.

Q14: Do they INSIST on doing periodical test restores of your backups to make sure the data is not corrupt and could be restored in the event of a disaster?

Your computer consultant should perform a monthly "fire drill" and perform a test restore from backup to make sure your data CAN be recovered in the event of an emergency. After all, the WORST time to "test" a backup is when you desperately need it.

Q15: Do they insist on backing up your network BEFORE performing any type of project or upgrade?

This is a simple precaution in case a hardware failure or software glitch causes a major problem.

Q16: If you were to experience a major disaster, do they have a written plan for how your data could be restored FAST and/or enable you to work from a remote location?

At minimum, you should have a simple disaster recovery plan for your data and network. I would also encourage you to do a full disaster recovery plan for your office, but at a minimum, your computer network will be covered should something happen.

Technical Expertise and Support:

Q17: Is their service-desk US based or outsourced to an overseas company or third party?

An in-house service desk helps ensure the people helping you are friendly and helpful. We consider this an important aspect of customer service, plus we feel it's important to keeping your data secure.

Q18: Do their technicians and engineers maintain current vendor certifications and participate in on-going training – or are they learning on your dime?

Any technician working on your network should be up to date on the vendor certifications on your network (i.e. Microsoft, Cisco, Dell, VMware, Citrix, etc.). Our experience is that the vast majority of technicians out there these days are woefully undertrained.

Q19: Do they arrive on time and dress professionally?

Any engineer working on your network is a part of your staff while at your facility. Are the engineers you're used to dealing with true professionals that you would be proud to have in your office? Do they dress professionally and show up on time?

Q20: Are they familiar with (and can they support) your unique line of business applications?

Any computer consultant should own the problems with all of your line of business applications. That doesn't necessarily mean that they can fix faulty software or be an expert trainer – but they SHOULD be the liaison between you and your vendor to resolve problems you are having and make sure these applications work smoothly for you.

Q21: When things wrong with your Internet, phones, printers or other IT services, do they say "that's not our problem to fix?"

Your computer consultant should own the problem so you don't have to try and resolve any of these issues on your own – that's just plain old good service and something many computer guys won't do.

The SuperSTAR Computer Consultant You Want vs A SuperSCREWup You Don't Want	
SuperSTAR Consultant	**SuperSCREWup Consultant**
Has proven qualifications and experience, is vendor certified	Is just getting started, has less than a year in business, has no tangible qualifications
Is fully insured (liability and worker's compensation)	Has no insurance
Has many client references and testimonials	Has no references or testimonials
Has multiple engineers	Has no backup team, works alone
Guarantees response times and has documented response systems in place (60 minutes or less)	Has no response system or guarantees, won't commit to anything
Documents all discussions, deliverables, guarantees and project timelines in writing	Prefers verbal communication, never follows up with written agreements
Uses detailed reporting	Provides no reports or status updates

SuperSTAR Consultant	SuperSCREWup Consultant
Has established offices and data centers	Has no office, uses a PO box and a cell phone
Provides all timelines, prices, and service level guarantees in writing	Provides vague project outlines, time and materials pricing, "window" timelines
Shows up on time	Shows up late or not at all
Sends correct, detailed invoices	Invoices are incorrect, never on time
Is easy to reach, returns calls promptly	Is hard to reach
Is always professionally dressed	Is sloppy, poorly dressed with a disheveled appearance
Uses systematic follow-up to ensure your satisfaction	Uses no follow-up, never hear from him unless you call with a problem
Solves problems quickly and professionally, stands behind all work for complete customer satisfaction	Is apathetic toward problem resolution, has no policies or procedures for resolving problems

12 Warning Signs that You Hired the Wrong Consultant

The consultant:

1. Becomes defensive or argumentative when you ask about project costs or completion dates, or when you question his recommendations.

2. Won't guarantee the work or your satisfaction.

3. Talks down to you, uses "geek speak," and makes you feel stupid when you question his recommendations or work.

4. Is consistently late or rushed, and misses deadlines without an explanation or apology.

5. Leaves your office a mess (wires and cables exposed, furniture out of place).

6. Looks sloppy or disheveled.

7. Uses high-pressure or scare tactics to get you to buy.

8. Doesn't explain your options for resolving a problem or completing a project; it's basically his way or the highway.

9. Doesn't follow up after completing a project.

10. Doesn't follow up after completing a project.

11. Never takes a proactive approach to supporting your network, and doesn't offer recommendations to help you secure your network, save money or improve your company's productivity.

12. Doesn't offer a preventive-maintenance or monitoring program to ensure that your network is protected from viruses, hackers, data loss, downtime or other problems.

5 More Mistakes to Avoid When Choosing a Computer Consultant

1. **Choosing a computer consultant based on a single phone call.** We recommend you invite them into your office and ask them for a <u>written</u> proposal. Be clear on what your expectations are and what type of problems you want them to resolve. A competent professional should offer to do an audit of your network to diagnose your system BEFORE quoting you anything. After all, would you take a doctor's word that you need surgery if they hadn't done x-rays or other diagnostics? Of course not! Prescription without diagnosis is malpractice.

2. **Choosing a computer consultant that doesn't have a written money-back guarantee**. In our view, a good consulting firm should be accountable for their services and fixing things RIGHT. If you aren't pleased with a job that was done, they should (at a minimum) make it right for free; and if they simply cannot resolve an issue to YOUR satisfaction, you shouldn't get stuck with the bill.

   Plus, the fact that they stand behind their work with a money-back guarantee shows they have confidence in themselves to make you a happy client. And don't fall for the, "We don't offer one because people will take advantage of us," routine. In our experience, MOST people just want an honest service at a reasonable price. If you give them that, they are happy to pay. Are there a few unethical folks out there? Of course, but they are the minority, and we would rather bite the bullet on the very few dishonest folks so we can gain the trust and confidence of the majority of clients who just want their problems fixed fast and fixed right.

3. **Choosing a computer consultant without speaking to several of their current clients**. Check their references! Don't just take the sales guy's word that they are good – ask to speak to at least 3 or 4 clients that are similar in size and scope to you. If they hesitate or cannot provide you with references, don't hire them!

   Another good sign is that they should have multiple client testimonials and success stories posted on their web site and throughout their marketing collateral. A lack of this may be a sign that they don't HAVE clients who are happy enough to provide a good reference – again, a warning sign.

4. **Choosing a computer consultant who cannot remotely monitor, update and support your network**. In this day and age, a computer consultant who doesn't do this is living in the stone ages. You want someone to do this because it will dramatically increase your network's security and will enable them to do faster repairs. That's not to say they shouldn't come onsite; but remote monitoring and repairs make fixing problems FASTER for YOU and help AVOID problems from cropping up in the first place.

5. **Choosing a computer consultant who isn't a major proponent of cloud technology**. If the computer consultant downplays, belittles, or dismisses the cloud, you know you are dealing with either an amateur or a consultant that's living in denial whose business is headed the way of the buggy whip manufacturers. By 2020, industry analysts project 88% of all business computing will be consumed on a pay-per use cloud model. This is a very good thing for the small and medium business owner. First, the recurring cycle of writing a big check for rip and replace IT upgrades, every 3 to 5 years, is gone.

Second, your IT will always run like new. Reputable cloud products, like TOSS C3's, IT as a Utility®, are built on extremely powerful technology capable of handling 10's of thousands of users without skipping a bit. Finally, worries about cyber-security, business continuity, and data loss are fears of the past. Data encryption, robust backup and disaster recovery, along with fully managed firewalls and intrusion prevention systems are all included in a solid cloud platform like IT as a Utility®.

Chapter Four

Avoiding Disasters & Expensive Miscommunications

If you've ever been disappointed with a computer consultant's service, this chapter will be of great interest to you.

Small technical "glitches" or repairs can be incredibly frustrating because they seem so insignificant, yet they greatly interfere with your ability to get things done. In most cases, business owners may be under the assumption that these tiny problems can be solved quickly, which is not always the case.

If you've hired an incompetent consultant before, you know that simple projects can turn into a full-day ordeal, and may even drag out for a week or more. Unbelievably, your small repair can end up requiring multiple follow-up visits and calls because it occurs repeatedly, even after it has been "fixed." To make matters worse, the consultant will probably charge you for those extra visits, even if the issue should have been resolved the first time you paid him to fix it!

This doesn't even take into consideration the inconvenience and downright chaos this causes to your business. Unlike automobile and home repairs, computer network problems can completely disrupt your business, taking you offline for hours or even days.

Consider this scenario:

You hire a consultant to upgrade your network, but he is way over deadline, and you are still experiencing problems; only now, he isn't returning your calls promptly and is acting as if YOU are the problem. Then, to add insult to injury, he asks you for more money!

While you're sitting there waiting for your network to come back online or your project to be completed, your stress level is escalating through the roof because you know your deadlines and clients aren't going to wait, and it further irritates you that the consultant has not kept the promises he so enthusiastically assured you of in the beginning.

Let's face it: You have a business to run, and you don't have the time to deal with technical issues or the incompetence of your consultant. Maybe you have a big proposal that needs to be submitted by the end of the day. Maybe you have sales leads or client orders that are getting colder by the minute and possibly even ruining client relationships. And, if you're like most business owners, you are already working behind schedule, so computer problems magnify the stress and delays to a whole new level.

If you've ever been through this type of nightmare, you know I'm not exaggerating. To prevent this from happening to you, or to avoid it happening again, you have to identify what causes these situations in the first place. That's what this chapter is all about.

Determine Your Priorities

The first step to avoiding problems with a computer consultant is to determine your "satisfaction priorities." Do you place a greater importance on response times or price? Is the quality of the work more important, or do you need it done fast? Is it critical that you have regular updates and status reports on your network, or is a quick e-mail now and again sufficient?

This is not to say that you can't have it all; but if fast response is a priority, you need to clearly communicate that to your computer consultant *before* you hire him. You should also detail what you consider "fast" to mean.

Do you expect him to return your call within 15 minutes or 2 hours? Do you expect him to be on-site the same day you call, or within the week? Make sure you are both clear before entering into an agreement. Some computer consulting firms may be more expensive, but may offer a higher quality of workmanship and customer service. Is that acceptable to you? Again, you need to determine this before entering into any project or agreement.

Once you've made a list of the qualities and characteristics that are most important to you, share this list with your prospective consultant to help him customize his services to suit you.

A Quick Word on Price

As with everything in life, you get what you pay for. The most expensive computer consultant will not necessarily be the best, but you should be cautious if your #1 priority is price. As a consumer, you know firsthand that you are always being offered competitive pricing on services and products. Businesses compete hard for your dollars and it's only natural for you to think of price first when looking for computer repair and consulting services.

However, services can't usually be compared like tangible goods such as cars or office equipment. With products, you can equate features and benefits in an apples-to-apples comparison. With services, there are too many intangible aspects that can't be compared easily.

If what you really want is cheap computer support, you can practically guarantee that you're going to have problems. The price won't seem so attractive when you've lost every file on your computer, or if the work has to be redone when it's discovered that it wasn't completed right in the first place.

If you rely heavily on your computer network and the information it contains, it only makes sense to take time and choose the most *competent* consultant possible, not the cheapest. Quality consultants can give you the expert advice and support you need. They can help lower your company's costs while increasing productivity, customer service and sales. And they will be there when you need them.

Start Small

Before you hire your computer consultant to install a new network, hire him to do a small repair or network audit. This will give you the opportunity to see if he shows up on time, follows through, and is enjoyable to work with. Never jump into a major project until you've been happy with the consultant's work on a smaller project.

Demand a Fixed Price

Many computer consultants charge by the hour for projects instead of quoting a fixed rate. This works great for them, but is dangerous for you. Unless you have an established, high-trust relationship with your consultant (or a bottomless pit of money,) never agree to this type of contract. This gives your consultant a wide-open field to take as long as he wants working on your project—and it actually benefits him if he does. Instead, ask him for a fixed fee that details exactly what results he will deliver for an agreed budget.

Get Everything in Writing

Getting everything in writing is one of the most important things you can do to avoid getting taken advantage of by an incompetent or less-than-ethical consultant. This includes:

- A project timeline and completion date
- A written service guarantee
- An exact budget and payment schedule
- Any and all expectations you have for deliverables
- When and how you will receive project updates

- Your responsibilities as the client
- What happens if you are not satisfied
- What happens if your project runs over the designated completion date

Do Your Research

We've discussed what to look for—actually demand—from your computer consultant. Some of those characteristics will need to be researched; don't skip those steps to save time. Ask your prospective consultant to provide the information you are looking for as part of his proposal. If he doesn't, or won't, cross him off your list of potential partners.

Communicate Your Concerns

Some people are too shy to say what's really on their mind for fear of appearing rude or unreasonable. But if you have any concerns, questions or reservations, you need to voice them to your prospective consultant before signing the contract, and ask him to address *in the contract* how he will overcome those concerns if you hire him for the project.

If you are concerned that he won't return your calls fast enough, let him know. If you are afraid he might not be able to handle the job, be honest and tell him. You don't have to be harsh or disagreeable; simply let him know that you have a few concerns and ask what he can do to assure you that you won't be disappointed.

Chapter Five

Getting the Most Out of Your Computer Consultant

Now that we've defined what to look for in qualified, competent, honest consultants, it makes sense to tell you how to get the most out of your relationship with them.

A great computer consultant will free you from worrying about data loss, downtime or other problems, allowing you to focus on the more important, strategic aspects of running and growing your business. It will also free your staff from trying to be jacks-of-all-trades and wasting time on activities they are not particularly good at, which also distracts them from doing their regular job. Ultimately, the consultant will recommend products and solutions to help your business operate more competitively, increase sales and lower your workload and stress levels. That's not to say you are completely off the hook.

There are a number of ways you can undo everything your consultant has done for you and severely jeopardize the security and reliability of your network. Plus, you are ultimately responsible for making sure your consultant understands your business priorities, goals and operational systems so he can offer advice and solutions to support you.

Once you understand your role and responsibilities for maximizing your technology investments, and what your consultant is and is not responsible for, you will have a much better working relationship with him and prevent most unpleasant surprises and expensive misunderstandings.

Take Responsibility for Your Own Protection

Many business owners automatically blame their computer or their consultant when they experience a problem, get infected with a virus, or realize their network has been taken over by spyware. And, in some cases, these problems *may be* due to negligence by your consultant.

However, most spyware and virus attacks are the result of an end-user downloading a questionable file or program, disabling their antivirus software, or somehow circumventing security settings or acceptable-use policies set by your consultant (such as visiting a peer-to-peer file-sharing network like uTorrent).

Many other problems are due to hardware or software inadequacies that can't be controlled or prevented by your consultant. And finally, many business owners don't want to pay for their consultants to perform simple preventive maintenance, update security patches and virus definitions, or monitor their system's performance. This lack of maintenance is an invitation for problems that can't be blamed on your computer consultant.

Unless your consultant has *complete* control over your network and has been given the responsibility to monitor and maintain your network 24/7/365, chances are that your problems were not caused directly by some action he took (or didn't take). Again, that is not to say that you are completely at fault for all network problems, but you and your employees need to take an active role in keeping your network and data safe from harm.

Keep Spyware, Malware and Viruses Off Your Network

In almost every case, malware, spyware and viruses are able to invade a network because of some action taken by a user. Cybercriminals are *incredibly clever* and have figured out ways to access your computer network through some of the most innocent and common activities you perform daily.

For example, many of the clients we see infected with spyware simply downloaded a screen saver, an "enhanced" Web browser, a music file, or some other "cute" program. In doing so, they also unknowingly downloaded a number of spyware and malware programs. Within a short time, they could no longer use their computer because of its slowness, instability and pop-ups. Your consultant can usually clean up the mess caused by these programs, but it is your responsibility to become educated about what you can and can't download. Below is a short list of programs and Websites you should never download or visit. Your consultant should be able to provide you with a more comprehensive, up-to-date list:

- Screen savers.
- "Enhanced" Web browsers like Cool Search.
- Emoticons.
- Games.
- Peer-to-peer file-sharing software (uTorrent).
- Music files.
- "For fun" surveys (what type of person are you?).
- Banners that challenge you to "punch the monkey," shoot something or answer a trivia question to win a prize.
- Sweepstakes or drawings.
- Any software that requires you to accept certain conditions; by agreeing to their conditions, usually outlined in small print, you are agreeing to accept third-party software.

Unfortunately, installing the above programs is not the only way a hacker or malware program can access your computer network. If you don't have the most up-to-date security patches and virus definitions installed, wrongdoers can access your computer through a banner ad or an e-mail attachment.

Over the past couple years, ransomware attacks have gained real momentum. These seemingly innocent downloads, grab all the drive letters and subsequently the folders and files within them, locks them down and encrypts them, rendering the data useless.

Your only recourse is to pay a "ransom" ranging from a few hundred dollars to 10's of thousands of dollars. There are two safeguards to protect against ransomware; regular full data backups and network based internet web filtering.

Be Aware Of Sneaky Ways Hackers Invade Your Network

Not too long ago, Microsoft released a security bulletin about three newly discovered vulnerabilities that could allow an attacker to gain control of your computer by tricking you into downloading and opening a maliciously crafted picture. At the same time, Microsoft released a Windows update to correct the vulnerabilities. But if you didn't have a process to ensure that you were applying critical updates as soon as they became available, you were completely vulnerable to this attack.

Here's another compelling reason to ensure your network stays up-to-date on the latest security patches: Most hackers do not discover these security loopholes on their own. Instead, they learn about them when Microsoft, or any other software vendor for that matter, announces the vulnerability and issues an update. That is the hackers' cue to spring into action; they immediately analyze the update and craft an exploit (like a virus) that allows them access to any computer or network that has not yet installed the security patch. The time between the release of the update and the release of the exploit that targets the underlying vulnerability is getting shorter every day.

When the "nimda" worm was first discovered in the fall of 2001, Microsoft had released the patch that protected against that vulnerability *331 days before.* So network administrators had plenty of time to apply the update. Of course, many still hadn't done so, and the nimda worm caused lots of damage. Now, as of March 2015, reports have shown that hackers can exploit vulnerabilities in less than a day, providing further proof that computer patches must be installed much more regularly than ever before.

Clearly, *someone* needs to be paying close attention to your systems to ensure that critical updates are applied as soon as possible. That's why we highly recommend that small-business owners without a full-time IT staff allow their consultant to monitor and maintain their network.

Create and Enforce an Acceptable-Use Policy (AUP)

An AUP is a written document stating exactly what your employees can and can't do with company Internet access, computers and e-mail. For example, employees should not be allowed to download or access programs, screen savers, pictures, music files or file-sharing networks. This will save precious bandwidth and prevent downloading viruses and spyware. An AUP should also educate employees on the appropriate use of your company's resources.

If you don't want your staff to download pornographic material and send racist jokes through a company e-mail account, you have to communicate this information to them in an acceptable-use policy and have them acknowledge *in writing* that they have read and understood it. Your consultant can help you draft this document and enforce the policies outlined.

Allow Your Consultant to Maintain Your Network

As we mentioned previously, many business owners do NOT perform regular maintenance on their computer network; they basically use the network until it stops working, and then bring in their consultant.

While this arrangement may seem to work just fine in the short-term, it can dramatically increase problems and the costs of keeping your network running. Then there is the threat of experiencing a major network disaster. Unfortunately, most businesses have to experience some type of catastrophe before they get serious about maintaining their network. Just ask any business owner about the importance of a solid backup or keeping their security up-to-date after they've gone through the devastation of losing a week's worth of work.

Look at these alarming statistics:

- Approximately **20%** of all small and medium-sized businesses endure a major network disaster every five years.
- The U.S. National Fire Protection Agency predicts that **43%** of companies that experience these disasters will never reopen, and another **29%** will close within three years.
- If the loss involves data, the diagnosis is even worse. According to the U.S. Bureau of Labor, **93%** of companies that suffer a significant data loss are out of business within five years.
- In April 2008, Symantec reported that there are over 1 million computer viruses in existence (and growing)
- The Internet Storm Center, https://isc.sans.edu, which tracks security attacks, reports **7.6 million attacks** in the U.S. alone.

If you really want to protect yourself from data loss, viruses, spyware, hackers, downtime and a host of other problems, the best thing you can do is find a computer consultant that offers 24/7/365 monitoring and maintenance for your network and cyber-security, and then let them do it for you. By allowing your consultant to control, manage and maintain your network, the chances of experiencing significant problems is greatly reduced (more on this in the following chapter).

Be a Great Client

There is a lot of truth in the cliché, "You'll attract more bees with honey than vinegar." This is especially true when working with professional consultants.

Quite often, business owners take an adversarial approach to working with their vendors. Since they are paying the bills, they believe that they have the right to be demanding, difficult and even hostile. What they don't realize is that vendor relationships can make or break a company, and maintaining a good working partnership with your computer consultant is critical to your business success.

The more respect and appreciation you give your consultant, the more he will want to do a great job for you. Keep in mind that you might need him to do you a favor, or pull you out of a big mess, somewhere down the road. If you've developed a good working relationship based on mutual trust and appreciation, he will be far more willing to go the extra mile and help you out when you need it most.

Here are three ways to make sure you become a "favorite" client who receives special favors and extra attention:

1. Pay all bills on time or early.
2. Express your appreciation for the work he's done. Everyone likes to know that their efforts are noticed.
3. If you have a complaint, don't jump to the conclusion that your consultant was trying to harm you on purpose. Let him know about your complaint and give him a chance to make it right before you get angry or take action. It may have been a simple mistake, or even an oversight, on *your* part.

Overall, clear communication is your best tool to ensure a great working relationship with your computer consultant. You want to find someone you can partner with long-term who will take an active role in making your business profitable and successful. That requires mutual respect on both sides.

Six Ways a Good Relationship with A Competent Computer Consultant Benefits Your Company

1. The consultant proactively monitors and maintains your network to prevent problems from happening, which gives you peace of mind by knowing that the "gremlins at the gate" are being watched and kept at bay.
2. The consultant is familiar with your network and therefore can troubleshoot problems faster.
3. He understands your business and can recommend ways to save money, increase productivity, reduce mistakes and service customers that you haven't even considered.
4. He helps lay a foundation for growing your business.
5. He knows about any software or hardware that has been added to your network (which are frequently the source of a problem).
6. He sorts through all the new technological breakthroughs, threats and news, and only informs you of the things you need to know.

Chapter Six

Preventing Disasters with Proactive Maintenance

The computers in your office and the network they serve are, without a doubt, the single most important tools you use on a daily basis to run your business. Your computer network is at the core of your communications, operations, accounting, client care and marketing. Just try to imagine one task or operation in your business that doesn't, directly or indirectly, depend on the security and availability of your computer network.

Yet, as important as your network is to your business, very few small-business owners take the necessary steps to ensure that it runs as smoothly and efficiently as possible. This is a huge, costly mistake.

With the constant changes to technology and daily development of new threats, even small peer-to-peer computer networks need ongoing maintenance and security updates from a highly trained consultant.

Unfortunately, what we see most business owners doing is ignoring regular maintenance and only calling a consultant when the network becomes inoperable. This reactive model of upkeep is a surefire path to extensive downtime, lost data and over spending on IT support, not to mention major disruptions in worker productivity, sales, cash flow, production and customer service that can never be recovered.

How Managed Services Can Prevent These Disasters from Happening to Your Business

Thanks to advances in technology, your computer consultant can now provide ongoing remote maintenance and support to maximize the performance, reliability and stability of your network.

The industry term for this is "managed services," although your consultant might have a different name for it.

The basic premise is this: For a fixed monthly fee, your computer consultant will take over the responsibility of performing regularly scheduled maintenance on your network to ensure that your virus protection and security patches are up-to-date, your backups are working properly, your firewall and other security settings are actively protecting you, the speed and performance of your network are maximized, and all the components of your network are functioning properly.

In essence, they are taking over the tactical, day-to-day maintenance and support of your network for a fraction of the cost of hiring a full-time consultant.

What Are The Benefits Of Managed Services?

Service calls to computer networks not under a managed-service plan (MSP) require two to three times as long to diagnose and repair as systems that are under a MSP, because of the time required for diagnostics and testing. This naturally leads to higher repair bills and more downtime.

In addition to the added expense and hours required for these repairs, some of the damage to your network can be irreversible, and could have been easily prevented with a solid MSP.

If the data and operation of your network is important to your business, you need to make sure you are taking the necessary steps to ensure its safety and security. A good managed-service plan will provide the following benefits:

- **You'll practically eliminate expensive repairs and data recovery costs.** By detecting and preventing network disasters before they happen, a good MSP will save you thousands of dollars in repairs and downtime.

- **You'll receive faster support**. Thanks to remote-monitoring software, your consultant will be able to securely access and repair most network problems right over the Internet. No more waiting around for an engineer to show up or paying for travel fees.

- **You'll experience faster performance, fewer problems and practically zero downtime.** Some components of your network will degrade in performance over time, causing it to slow down, hang up and crash. The regular preventive maintenance offered through an MSP will make sure your computers stay in tip-top shape for maximum speed, performance and reliability.

- **You'll get top-level IT support without the costs and overhead of hiring a full-time IT manager.** A junior technician can easily cost your company $45,000-50,000 a year in salary, taxes and insurance, and a senior consultant could cost two to three times that amount. Under an MSP, you get to share a senior consultant with other businesses, which greatly reduces your costs without sacrificing experience or quality of work.

- **You'll receive discounts on new projects and better service.** Most computer consultants will offer priority service and a discount to clients on their managed-service plan. Plus, your consultant will become more familiar with your hardware, software, settings and history, and therefore provide faster service than the consultant who has to spend time "feeling around" your network.

- **You can budget for IT support just like rent or insurance.** If your IT support bill varies from month to month, a managed-service plan will help even it out and make budgeting easier. Just make sure the plan you sign up for is all-inclusive, with no hidden charges, caveats or fees.

- **You will safeguard your data.** The data on the hard disk is always more important than the hardware that houses it. If you rely on your computer system for daily operations, it's time to get serious about protecting your critical, irreplaceable electronic information. A good MSP will greatly reduce your chances of losing critical company data, files and information.
- **You'll gain peace of mind.** As a business owner, you already have enough to worry about; the last thing you need is a computer crisis. Having a managed-service plan in place takes that worry off your plate.

What to Look For In A Managed-Service Plan

There are a number of factors to look for in a MSP. A good consultant will take time to sit down with you and explain your options, based on your priorities, budget, network complexity, support needed and conditions of satisfaction. However, here are a few things to make sure your consultant includes in your agreement:

- **Security Patches and Updates.** Software vendors frequently issue critical patches to cover known security loopholes in their software. However, not all patches are trouble-free, and some will require specialized knowledge to install. On many occasions, Microsoft has distributed patches that come with fine-print instructions warning the user to install and test the patch on one machine before rolling it out to all the computers on the network. Since most people don't read the fine print on a software download, or are simply not aware of the problems that can arise from installing an untested patch, they blindly install it on their entire network only to discover that it caused a number of software conflicts and system failures. That's why it makes sense to allow a trained professional to manage and install patches on a regular basis. Trying to do this on your own is similar to playing Russian roulette with your network.

- **24/7/365 Monitoring and Alerts.** Your consultant should be able to provide around-the-clock monitoring for your network to look for problems developing under the radar. He should also notify you of problems in advance so that preventive action can be taken.
- **Spam Filtering.** Not only is spam annoying, it is the number-one way viruses enter a computer network.
- **Virus Updates.** Unless you've been living under a rock, you know that viruses are a real, and very dangerous, threat to your computer network. Since new viruses launch daily, you need to make sure your consultant is also monitoring your virus protection, and automatically updating your network with new virus definitions as soon as they become available. **Note:** Your consultant will often recommend virus software for you to purchase; it is not normally included in a MSP.
- **Spyware Scanning and Removal.** Like viruses, spyware can cause a number of problems for your network and may even result in identity theft. Symptoms of spyware include excessive pop-up ads, sluggish performance, and strange Web browsers opening on your computer that you did not request.
- **System Backup Monitoring.** Your consultant should monitor your daily system backups to make sure they are working properly, and perform a monthly test

restore to make sure your data is available in a usable format. Tape backups are notorious for failing. Even if they appear to be working, the data could be corrupt and useless. We have seen several situations where a company thought their data was secure only to find out that it wasn't when they desperately needed it. Some consultants will even offer an off-site data backup solution.

- **Vendor Liaison.** Quite often, software or hardware will just fail. It's far more convenient to have a consultant who is familiar with your network to deal with the warranty returns and replacements of those parts with the manufacturer, rather than deal with it yourself. If you've ever had to call the "customer service" hotline of a technology vendor, you know what a headache it can be. Other vendors include practice-management software, Internet providers, Web-hosting companies, and so on. For convenience, have your consultant agree to be your vendor liaison with these companies so you don't have the hassle.

- **Creation of Acceptable-Use Policies and Training.** An acceptable-use policy is simply the rulebook for what your employees can and can't do with their computers. Uneducated employees can accidentally introduce spyware, viruses, hackers and other major problems into your network. They can also use their work computer and e-mail to access and share unacceptable material. All it takes is one employee to send an off-color joke to a list of friends from your company's e-mail to start problems for you. In some cases, employees' actions can bring expensive and embarrassing lawsuits against your company. Talk to your consultant about ways to educate and enforce an acceptable-use policy.

- **Adding and Removing Hardware and Software.** You just purchased a new printer and you're eager to start using it. However, you can't figure out why you keep getting error messages and why you can't print from Excel. If you had a managed-service contract that covered hardware and software installation, your consultant would be responsible for making sure it was installed and configured properly, and you wouldn't have to waste one minute dealing with these problems.

- **Adding and Removing Users.** Although this seems like a simple thing, user access to your network is a critical security risk that needs to be managed properly to avoid disgruntled employees or unauthorized persons accessing it. This is especially true if you have remote workers.

- **Help Desk Support.** This would include a mix of phone, remote and on-site support for you and your employees to answer any number of technical questions and problems. Remember, phone support is not free; calling your consultant for a "quick" question is a billable event and can cost you $25-100. Therefore, you want to have some level of remote and on-site support included in your managed-service contract.

Keep in mind that this is just a starter list of services to look for. The size and complexity of your network, the security required, and the software and systems you use will largely determine the type of ongoing support you need. A good computer consultant will take time to understand your needs and offer multiple plans to choose from. He will also be flexible and allow you to upgrade or downgrade the level of support provided if you discover that your plan is not meeting your needs.

Managed Security Service Plans

Cyber-security threats are in the news daily. The need for a security specialist is no longer a nice to have, it is a must. If ethics, compliance, and security of your data and business are important, then you must purchase a solid Managed Security Service Plan, (MSSP), tailored specifically to your company's requirements. The main security services you need to consider are: Managed Firewall Service, Managed Intrusion Detection and Prevention Systems, Managed VPNs, Managed Antivirus Protection, Managed Endpoint Threat Protection, Managed Authentication and Identification Services, Managed Content Filtering, DDoS Protection, and Ongoing Vulnerability Assessment.

5 Things to Look For in a Managed Security Service Provider

1. A qualified security provider will run and manage its own Security Operations Center, (SOC), and have a Security Information and Event Management, (SEIM), system in place, working 24/7/365. SIEM technology works in real-time, providing analysis of alerts generated by network hardware and applications and us critical in sifting through the terabytes of raw data.

2. Establish expectations of the relationship. Consider the services and expertise required for the security program. Evaluate the strength of each vendor, choosing an MSSP that most closely matches your company's needs.

3. Select an MSSP that sets clear expectations about the client requirements. Roles and responsibilities for the MSSP and the client should be clearly spelled out.

4. A tailored solution designed specifically for your company can increase the overall IT security. Look for an MSSP willing to propose a solution based on your specific requirements. In addition to a customized solution,

consider a service provider who can provide the total package, i.e. service, software, hardware, and support.

5. An emergency response team that can provide forensic analysis when attacks occur and when vulnerabilities are assessed.

Chapter Seven

Moving to the Cloud

Undoubtedly you've heard all the commotion around cloud computing and how it's the "next big thing." Yet, despite all the hype, no one really seems to understand what cloud computing is or how it can help your business.

That's why we wanted to set the record straight and provide business owners and executives a simple, easy to read report that would explain what cloud computing is, how it can (possibly) help your business and if so, what you need to know in order to make good decisions about which vendor to choose.

Why "possibly," because cloud computing may NOT be a good fit for every company; and if you don't get all the facts or fully understand the pros and cons, you can end up making some VERY poor and expensive decisions that you'll deeply regret later.

That said, for some clients, cloud can actually lower their IT costs by 20% - 50%, greatly improve the ability for remote workers to connect and work, simplify their entire IT infrastructure and genuinely solve a number of technology problems that they've been trying to work around for years.

So which are YOU? By the end of this chapter you'll know, or at least have a much better understanding. Of course, we are always available as a resource for a second opinion or quick question, so please feel free to contact my office directly if we can clarify any points made in this report or answer any questions you have.

5 Critical Facts You Must Know Before Moving to the Cloud

In this chapter I'm going to talk about 5 very important facts you need to know before considering cloud computing for your company.

1. What cloud computing is.
2. The pros AND cons of this new technology.
3. The various types of cloud computing options you have (there is more than just one).
4. Answers to important, frequently asked questions you need to know.
5. What questions you need to ask your IT pro before letting them "sell" you on moving all or part of your network and applications to the cloud.

I've also included some actual case studies from other businesses that have moved to cloud computing, along with several sample cost comparison chart so you can see the impact this new technology can have on your business and IT budget.

What Is Cloud Computing?

Wikipedia defines cloud computing as, "The use and access of multiple server-based computational resources via a digital network (WAN, Internet connection using the World Wide Web, etc.)."

But what does that mean?

The easiest way to not only understand what cloud computing is but also gain insight into why it's gaining in popularity, is to compare it to the evolution of public utilities. For example, let's look at the evolution of electricity.

Back in the industrial age, factories had to produce their own power in order to run machines that produced the hard goods they manufactured. Be it textiles or railroad spikes, using machines gave these companies enormous competitive advantages by producing more goods with fewer workers and in less time. For many years, the production of power was every bit as important to their company's success as the skill of their workers and quality of their products.

Unfortunately, this put factories into TWO businesses: the business of producing their goods and the business of producing power. Then the concept of delivering power (electricity) as a utility was introduced by Thomas Edison when he developed a commercial-grade replacement for gas lighting and heating using centrally generated and distributed electricity. From there, as they say, the rest is history.

The concept of electric current being generated in central power plants and delivered to factories as a utility caught on quickly. This meant manufacturers no long had to be in the business of producing their own power. In fact, in a very short period of time, it became a competitive necessity for factories to take advantage of the lower cost option being offered by public utilities. Almost overnight, thousands of steam engines and electric generators were rendered obsolete and left to rust next to the factories they used to power.

What made this possible was a series of inventions and scientific breakthroughs – but what drove the demand was pure economics. Utility companies were able to leverage economies of scale that single manufacturing plants simply couldn't match in output or in price. In fact, the price of power dropped so significantly that it quickly became affordable for not only factories but every single household in the country.

Today, we are in a similar transformation following a similar course. The only difference is that instead of cheap and plentiful electricity, advancements in technology and Internet connectivity are driving down the costs of computing power. With cloud computing, businesses can pay for "computing power" like a utility without having the exorbitant costs of installing, hosting, maintaining, upgrading, and supporting it.

In fact, you are probably already experiencing the benefits of cloud computing in some way but hadn't realized it. Below are a number of cloud computing applications, also called SaaS or "software as a service," you might be using:

- Gmail, Hotmail or other free e-mail accounts
- Facebook
- NetSuite, Salesforce
- Constant Contact, Exact Target, Aweber or other e-mail broadcasting services
- Zoomerang, SurveyMonkey and other survey tools
- LinkedIn
- Twitter
- All things Google (search, AdWords, maps, etc.)
- iCloud, DropBox, EverNote and other storage services

If you think about it, almost every single application you use today can be (or already is) being put "in the cloud" where you can access it and pay for it via your browser for a monthly fee or utility pricing. You don't purchase and install software but instead access it via an Internet browser.

What about Office 365 and Google Apps?

Office 365 and Google Apps are perfect examples of the cloud computing trend. For an inexpensive monthly fee, you can get full access and use of Office applications that used to cost a few hundred dollars or more to purchase. Additionally, since these apps are being powered by the cloud provider, you don't need an expensive desktop with lots of power to use them – just a simple Internet connection will do on a laptop, desktop, tablet, or mobile device.

Of course, these aren't great options for all businesses. Google Apps doesn't integrate with many line-of-business applications, which presents a deal breaker for using this service. For example, if you like using Microsoft's Excel or Word to pull reports or create documents from your line of business application, you might not be able to do that with Google Apps. Gmail, Google's answer to Microsoft's Exchange server and Outlook combination, is very free-form and open. Many of our clients who have tried Gmail quickly become frustrated and request to return to Outlook.

Microsoft's Office 365 is a great platform for some companies and due to key limitations, make it a poor choice for many businesses, not to mention that customers get near-zero help desk support. The limitations pop-up quickly once you need to implement a non-Microsoft technology with your "servers" in the Office 365 Cloud with Azure. For example, if you have a line of business application such as QuickBooks, TABS3, ProLaw, or Autonomy which require fast access to your servers, Microsoft is not going to install a dedicated custom system for you or anyone else, since it does not fit their "cookie cutter model." If something goes wrong, there isn't a customer service help desk that offers immediate support or assistance. But again, it's a perfect example of where the industry is headed to anticipate the needs for cloud computing.

Here's an interesting set of questions to ponder while considering these or any cloud based solution. Where will my data reside? Will my data ever leave the United States? How many copies of my data will be out in the cloud? Who will have physical access to my data? Who is responsible for backing up my data and how will I recover it when necessary? If I decide to switch providers, how will my data be properly destroyed along with all copies, and what guarantee will I have that my data was properly destroyed?

Pros and Cons of Moving to the Cloud

As you read this section, keep in mind there is no "perfect" solution. All options – be it an in-house network or a cloud solution – have both upsides and downsides. Your selection has to be determined on a case-by-case scenario before you can come to a complete conclusion on which option will work best for you. (Warning: Do not let a cloud expert tell you there is only "one way" of doing something.) Some companies end up with a hybrid solution where some of their applications are in the cloud and some are still hosted and maintained from an in-house system. We'll discuss more of this in a later section. Here are the general pros and cons of cloud computing:

Pros of Cloud Computing:

- **Lowered IT costs.** Lowered IT costs. This is probably the single most compelling reason why companies choose to move their network (all or in part) to the cloud. You'll save money on software licenses, hardware (servers, laptops, and workstations) as well as on IT support and upgrades. In fact, we save our clients an average of 20% to 50% when we move some or all of their network functionality to the cloud.

- **So if you hate constantly writing big, fat checks for IT upgrades**, you'll really want to look into cloud computing. Later in this report, are examples of how we've done this for other clients and what the savings have been.

- **Ability to access your desktop and/or applications from anywhere on any device.** If you travel a lot, have remote workers or prefer to use an iPad while traveling, a laptop at your house, and a PC from the office, then cloud computing will give you the ability to work from any of these devices. This benefit of work any time, from anywhere, on any device, consistently ranks as a top 3 benefit from all client and market surveys TOSS C3 conducts.

- **Disaster recovery and backup are automated**. The servers in your office are extremely vulnerable to a number of threats including viruses, human error, hardware failure, software corruption, power outage, and, of course, physical damage due to a fire, flood or other natural disaster. If your servers were in the cloud and your office was reduced to a pile of rubble, you could purchase a new laptop and be back up and running immediately. This would NOT be the case if you had a traditional in-house network and were using tape drives, CDs, USB drives, online backup services, or standard disk to disk devices to back up your system.

- Synonymous to a public utility, cloud platforms are far more robust and secure than your average business network, because they utilize economies of scale to invest heavily into security, redundancy, and failover systems making them far less likely to go down. This in itself is a budget saver. The dollars being spent now on backup services, tapes, and the cost of downtime when a recovery is required, are all returned back to the bottom-line.

- **It's faster, cheaper, and easier to set up new employees.** If you have a seasonal workforce or a lot of turnover, cloud computing will not only lower your costs of setting up new accounts, but it will make it infinitely faster. "TOSS C3 currently provides cloud IT for a local firm that brings on an average of 10 extra summer interns in May through August. If they had a traditional network setup, they would have to purchase expensive PCs and software licenses for these temporary workers and then pay to maintain and upgrade them throughout the year. Using cloud computing, these interns use their own laptops and log into the network securely. The firm ONLY pays for those workers' licenses during the time when they are interning, just like a utility. When September comes around, they no longer pay for those licenses and support. Using this model saves them approximately $27,000 a year in hardware, software and IT services."

- **You use it without having to "own" it.** More specifically, you don't own the responsibility of having to install, update, and maintain the infrastructure. Think of it similar to living in a condo where someone else takes care of the building maintenance, repairing the roof, and mowing the lawn, but you still have the only key to your section of the building and use of all the facilities. This is particularly attractive for companies who are new, expanding, or facing a major IT upgrade, and don't want the heavy outlay of cash for purchasing and supporting an expensive computer network. Simply put, IT as a Utility®, takes the variable Capital (CAPEX), Operating (OPEX), and Human Resource expenses you are pouring into IT, off of your income statement and balance sheet and replaces them with a predictable and scalable single line-item under your monthly utility (IT) expenses.

- **It's a "greener" technology that will save on power and your electric bill.** For some smaller companies, the power savings will be too small to measure. However, for larger companies with multiple servers who are cooling a hot server room and keeping their servers running 24/7/365, the savings are considerable. One of our clients had 4 cabinets of servers and storage costing them $4,700.00 on average per month for power and cooling, which was eliminated when they moved to the cloud.

- **It's an "offsite" system that will save on real-estate costs.** Real-estate is expensive and with the economy turning around, the cost per square foot won't be coming down any time soon. Smaller companies can reclaim the server room and put it to better use while larger companies can reclaim large areas or an entire floor, not to mention the expensive rent being spent on co-location facilities and other redundant offsite locations and data centers.

Cons of Cloud Computing:

- **The Internet going down.** While you can mitigate this risk by using a commercial grade Internet connection and maintaining a secondary backup connection, there is a chance that you'll lose Internet connectivity, making it difficult to work from the office. You'll find more information about this under the "FAQ's About Security, Where Your Data Is Held and Internet Connectivity" later on in this report.

- **Data security.** Many people don't feel comfortable having their data in some offsite location. This is a valid concern and before you choose any cloud provider, you need to find out more information about where they are storing your data, how it's encrypted, who has access to it, and how you can get it back. You'll find more information about this under the "What to Look for When Hiring a Cloud Integrator" later on in this document.

- **Certain line-of-business applications won't work in the cloud.** For example AutoCAD and 3D-rendering, some lab equipment and manufacturing systems that need a rapid high-speed interface between software and machinery. In Google or Office 365's cloud, in fact, no line of business application will work that is not part of their cloud offering.

- **Compliance Issues.** There are a number of laws and regulations such as Gramm-Leach-Bliley, Sarbanes-Oxley, and HIPAA that require companies to control and protect their data and certify that they have knowledge and control over who can access the data, who sees it and how, and where it is stored. In a public cloud environment, this can be a problem. Many cloud providers won't tell you specifically where your data is stored. In fact, Office i365 and Google truly have no knowledge of where your data is, physically.

- **Most cloud providers have certifications** which require them to be able to describe exactly what is happening in their environment, how and where the data comes in, what the provider does with it, and what controls are in place over the access to and processing of the data. As the business owner, it's YOUR neck on the line if the data is compromised, so it's very important that you ask for some type of validation that they are meeting the various compliance regulations on an ongoing basis.
- **Some key questions** you'll want to know the answers to are: Where is the data located? Who has access to it? How is the data being stored in production and in DR? Is the data encrypted in-flight and at rest? Is the company SSAE16 compliant? Is the company HIPAA compliant?
- **Intimate knowledge of your system for support.** When everything's working, the cloud is great. What happens when you can't access an application or your data? 24/7/365 support from knowledgeable engineers who know your company and your system is crucial. Nothing can be more frustrating than getting an overseas level-1 support tech who's reading from a prompter, following a generic script, and wasting your time and money.

Different Types Of Cloud Solutions Explained:

Pure Cloud: This is where all your applications and data are put on the other side of the firewall (in the cloud) and accessed through various devices (laptops, desktops, iPads, and mobile devices) via the Internet.

Hybrid Cloud: Although "pure" cloud computing has valid applications, for some, it can be a scary first step. A hybrid cloud enables you to put certain pieces of your existing IT infrastructure (say, Business Continuance and Disaster Recovery) in the cloud, while the remainder of the IT infrastructure stays on premise. This gives you the ability to enjoy the costs savings and benefits of cloud computing where it makes the most sense without the risk of being out of compliance, if you are in a highly regulated industry.

Point Solutions: Another option would be simply to put certain applications, like Microsoft Exchange, Email Encryption, CRM, or Accounting in the cloud while keeping everything else onsite. Since e-mail is usually a critical application that everyone needs and wants access to on the road and on various devices (iPad, smart phone, etc.) then often this is a great way to get advanced features of Microsoft Exchange without the cost of installing and supporting your own in-house Exchange Server, Operating System, and Licensing.

Public Cloud vs. Private Cloud: Public Clouds are services that anyone can tap into with a network connection and a credit card. They are shared infrastructures that allow you to pay-as-you-go and managed through a self-service web portal. Private clouds are essentially custom built infrastructures that mimic public cloud services, but are on premise. Private clouds are often the choice of companies who want the benefits of cloud computing, but don't want their data held in a public or offsite environment. Another term used today for Private Clouds is Converged Infrastructure. If you are in a highly regulated industry, then a private or a hybrid cloud makes sense.

FAQs About Security, Where You Data Is Held And Internet Connectivity

Question: What if my Internet connection goes down for an extended period of time?

My Answer: While this is a valid concern, TOSS C3 offers a service called WAN-UP™ which takes two or more wired and or wireless internet services from different providers and connects them to the supplied 24/7 managed appliance. Once connected, the appliance will aggregate the bandwidth giving you full usage of all bandwidth purchased. In the event of an internet line failure, the appliance automatically routes your access to another available line. The result is super-fast access when all lines are up and not losing access if one internet line goes down. You can connect from 2 to 26 separate internet lines with WAN-UP™.

Question: What happens if we lose power or can't get to the office, how can we continue to work productively?

My Answer: One of the many problems our IT as a Utility® cloud platform solves, is continuous access from any device and from any location. Since you're IT infrastructure is liberated from your office, power outages, building shutdowns, storms, and other mishaps have zero impact on your IT system. This allows you and your staff to use any device that can get an internet connection and securely login into your IT as a Utility® system enabling you to conduct business as usual with no diminishment of service.

Question: What about security? Isn't there a big risk of someone accessing my data if it's in the cloud?

My Answer: In many cases, cloud computing is a MORE secure way of accessing and storing data. Just because your server is onsite doesn't make it more secure. In fact, most businesses can't justify the cost of securing their network the way a cloud provider can. Most security breaches occur due to human error; one of your employees downloads a file that contains a virus, they don't use secure passwords, or they simply e-mail confidential information out to people who shouldn't see it. Other security breaches occur in on-site networks because the company didn't properly maintain their own in-house network with security updates, software patches, and up-to-date anti-virus, and firewalls. That's a FAR more common way networks get compromised verses a cloud provider getting hacked. At TOSS C3, we use clusters of highly available firewalls, intrusion detection systems, and 2-factor authentication is available as an option. Additionally, all data at the production and Disaster Recovery facilities is encrypted both at rest and in-flight.

Question: Can someone tap into my cloud connection and read my email or get my data?

My Answer: Most providers have some form of encryption for your cloud connection that prevents this from happening. Your connection to TOSS C3's IT as a Utility® completely mitigates this by keeping all of the data, applications, and processing securely in the cloud data centers so your connection has no information within it other than video signaling, sound, keyboard strokes, and mouse movements. When you do download or print a file, the data is encrypted prior to sending it to you and the entire time it takes to get to your device, so security is not an issue.

Question: What if WE don't like the cloud? How do I get my data back?

My Answer: We give every client detailed information that clearly outlines where their data is and how they could get it back in the event of an emergency. This includes emergency contact numbers, information on how to access your data and infrastructure without needing our assistance (although we are always available to support you,) and information regarding your backups and licensing.

In fact, you should never hire ANY IT professional that won't give you that information. We also have the ability, with our vBCDR® system, to replicate your data every day to your office so you have a physical copy and back up of your entire network to guarantee that your applications, servers, and data are always accessible by you. vBCDR®, which stands for Virtual Business Continuity and Disaster Recovery, is a patent pending system TOSS C3 developed in conjunction with DELL and utilizes TOSS' Cloud on Write® technology. vBCDR® is an invaluable and robust optional service protecting files, folders, applications, servers, sites, and the enterprise.

Question: Do I have to purchase new hardware (servers, workstations) to move to the cloud?

My Answer: No! That's one of the best benefits of cloud computing. It allows you to use older workstations, laptops and servers because the computing power is in the cloud. Not only does that allow you to keep and use hardware longer, but it allows you to buy cheaper workstations and laptops because you don't need the expensive computing power required in the past. Ninety-nine percent of our clients use their existing equipment or low-cost laptops, and those who add additional systems, usually purchase cloud terminals, which are very low-cost purpose built appliances that boot directly into the cloud.

Question: What if the PC or Laptop I use to access the cloud dies, then what?

My Answer: The beauty of the cloud is that you can use any device as an endpoint. We recommend that our clients keep one or 2 low-cost systems on hand to swap out dead or crashed systems.

Of course, you can always pop down to Staples or Best-Buy and purchase a low cost PC or laptop in a pinch.

What to Look For When Hiring a Cloud Integrator

A "cloud integrator" is a fancy name for an IT consultant who helps you set up and integrate the various software and solutions into a cloud service specific for your business. But buyer beware! The cloud is still considered to be brand new technology and you don't want just anyone setting you up on this.

Unfortunately, the computer repair and consulting industry (along with many others) has its own share of incompetent or unethical people who will try to take advantage of trusting business executives who simply do not have the ability to determine whether or not they know what they are doing. Sometimes this is out of desire for your money; more often it's simply because they don't have the skills and competency to do the job correctly but won't tell you that up front because they want to make the sale.

From misleading information, unqualified technicians, and slack management, to terrible customer service and poorly performing systems, we've seen it all…and we know they exist in abundance because we have had a number of customers come to us to clean up the disasters they have caused.

Automotive repair shops, electricians, plumbers, lawyers, realtors, dentists, doctors, accountants, etc. are heavily regulated to protect the consumer from receiving substandard work or getting ripped off. However, the computer industry is still highly unregulated and there are few laws in existence to protect the consumer – which is why it's so important for you to really research the company or person you are considering to make sure they have the experience to set up, migrate, and support your network in the cloud.

Anyone who can hang out a shingle can promote themselves as a cloud expert. Even if they are honestly trying to do a good job for you, their inexperience can cost you dearly in your network's speed and performance or in lost or corrupt data files. To that end, here are 20 questions you should ask your IT person before letting them migrate your network to the cloud:

Critical Questions to Ask Your IT Company Or Computer Consultant BEFORE Letting Them Move Your Network To The Cloud

Q1: How many clients have you provided cloud services for to date and can you provide references?

My Answer: You don't want someone practicing on your network. At a minimum, make sure they have a minimum of 1,000 companies using some or all of their cloud services on a daily basis.

Q2: How quickly do they guarantee to have a technician working on an outage or other problem?

My Answer: Anyone you pay to support your network should give you an SLA (service level agreement) that outlines exactly how IT issues get resolved and in what time frame. I would also request that they reveal what their average resolution time has been with current customers over the last 3-6 months.

They should also answer their phones, be available for you 24/7, and provide you with an emergency number you may call if a problem arises at any time, especially on weekends.

If you cannot access your network because the Internet is down or due to some other problem, you can't be waiting around for hours for someone to call you back OR (more importantly) start working on resolving the issue. Make sure you get this in writing; often cheaper or less experienced consultants won't have this or will try and convince you it's not important or that they can't do this. Don't buy that excuse. They are in the business of providing IT support so they should have some guarantees or standards around this they can share with you.

Q3: What's your plan for transitioning our network to the cloud to minimize problems and downtime?

My Answer: We run your cloud environment for up to 30 days prior to the transition and don't "turn off" the old network until everyone is 100% confident that everything has been converted and is working effortlessly. You just don't want a company to switch you overnight without setting up a test environment first. This process ensures that all systems are functioning and tuned for maximum effectiveness. Once you approve of the cloud conversion, we perform a final non-disruptive off-hours data migration. On 'Go-Live' day, TOSS C3 schedules your engineering team to be available to make any needed adjustments and to answer questions that will come up within your organization.

Q4: Do they take the time to explain what they are doing and answer your questions in terms that you can understand (not geek speak), or do they come across arrogant and make you feel uneasy for asking simple questions?

My Answer: Our engineers are trained to have the 'heart of a teacher' and will take the time to answer your questions and explain everything in simple terms. Our clients consistently rate TOSS C3's service and engineers at a 9.3, on a scale of 1 to 10 with '10' being the highest possible score.

Q5: Where will your data be stored?

My Answer: You should receive full documentation about where your data is, how it's being secured and backed up, and how you could get access to it if necessary WITHOUT going through your provider. Essentially, you don't want your cloud provider to be able to hold your data (and your company) hostage.

Q6: How will your data be secured and backed up?

My Answer: If they tell you that your data will be stored in their own co-location facility, located in the back of their office, what happens if THEY get destroyed by a fire, flood or other disaster? What are they doing to secure the office and access? Are they backing it up somewhere else? Make sure they are certified and have a failover plan in place to ensure continuous service in the event that their location goes down. If they are building on another service provider's platform, you still want to find out where your data is and how it's being backed up. We take regular full backups, as snapshots, of your data, applications, and servers, no less than every 4 hours. These snapshots are then encrypted and replicated offsite to one of our other data center locations. Data security is critical to TOSS C3 and you can rest assured that you won't be reading about TOSS or your company's data breach in the newspaper.

Q7. What is THEIR disaster recovery plan? What happens if they go out of business?

My Answer: TOSS C3 is a profitable debt-free company which started operating in 1985. We have multiple data centers which we own and each is fully redundant at all levels. TOSS C3's disaster recovery plan is based around continuous operations for our clients and TOSS itself, as we are an IT as a Utility® client in the TOSS Cloud. Should you ever want your data back, a simple call to the Cloud Support Center initiates the process. We'll then work with your team to put your data on the most suitable media and have it delivered right to your door. After all, it is YOUR data.

Q8: Do they have adequate errors and omissions insurance as well as workers' compensation insurance to protect YOU?

My Answer: Here's something to consider, if THEY create a problem with your network that causes you to be down for hours or days or to lose data, who's responsible? Here's another question to consider, if one of their technicians gets hurt at your office, who's paying? In this litigious society we live in, you better make sure that whomever you hire is adequately insured with both errors and omissions insurance AND workers' compensation – and don't be shy about asking them.

True Story: A few years ago Geek Squad was slapped with multi-million dollar lawsuits from customers for the bad behavior of their technicians. In some cases, their techs where accessing, copying and distributing personal information they gained access to on customers' PCs and laptops brought in for repair. In other cases, they lost clients' laptops (and subsequently all the data on them) and tried to cover it up. Bottom line, make sure the company you are hiring has proper insurance to protect YOU.

Q9: Is it standard procedure for them to provide you with written system documentation detailing what software licenses you own, your critical passwords, user information, hardware inventory, etc., or are they the only ones with the "keys to the kingdom?"

My Answer: All clients receive this in electronic form, upon request, and at no additional cost. We also perform regular updates to this material. We also make certain that key people from your organization have this information and know how to use it, giving you complete control over your network.

Side Note: You should NEVER allow an IT person to have that much control over you and your company. If you get the sneaking suspicion that your current IT person is keeping this under their control as a means of job security, get rid of them (and we can help to make sure you don't suffer ANY ill effects). This is unethical and dangerous to your organization, so don't tolerate it!

Q10: Do they have other technicians on staff who are familiar with your network in case your regular technician goes on vacation or gets sick?

My Answer: Yes, and we always make a best effort to match you with your installation team; and since we keep detailed network documentation (basically a blueprint of your computer network) and updates on every client's account, if your team is not available, any of our engineers can pick up where another left off.

Q11: Do they INSIST on doing periodic test restores of your backups to make sure the data is not corrupt and could be restored in the event of a disaster?

My Answer: Backup and recovery is critical, so beyond our daily checking and testing, we perform a monthly test restore from backup for our clients to make sure their data CAN be recovered in the event of an emergency. Upon completion, we then send our clients a notification stating that this test restore was conducted and that all systems are a "go." If there's a problem, we notify our clients immediately and start working to resolve it the same day. After all, the WORST time to "test" a backup is when you desperately need to recover from it.

Q12: Is their help-desk US-based or outsourced to an overseas company or third party?

My Answer: We provide our own in-house, US-based help desk from our Cloud Support Center, and make sure the engineers are friendly and helpful. We consider this one of the most important aspects of customer service, and our existing clients send us a lot of praise and recognition for our responsiveness, friendliness, and knowledge. Additionally, keeping support for your IT systems in the US is an important first step in data security.

Q13: Do their technicians maintain current vendor certifications and participate in on-going training – or are they learning on your dime?

My Answer: Our engineers are required to keep the most up-to-date vendor certifications in all the software we support, especially Microsoft, VMware, and Citrix. Our hiring process is so stringent that 99% of the engineers who apply don't make it through. (Guess who's hiring them?)

Q14: Are they familiar with (and can they support) your unique line of business applications?

My Answer: We own the problems with all line of business applications for our clients. That doesn't mean we can fix faulty software – but we WILL be the liaison between you and your vendor to resolve problems you are having and make sure these applications work smoothly for you instead of pointing fingers and putting you in the middle. In fact, since 2001, TOSS C3 has successfully cloud converted every application we have been given that run on either a Microsoft or Linux platform.

Q15: When something goes wrong with your Internet service, IP phone systems, printers or other IT services, do they own the problem or do they say "that's not our problem to fix?"

My Answer: TOSS C3 believes that WE should own the problem for our clients so they don't have to try and resolve any of these issues on their own – that's just plain old good service and something many computer companies won't do.

Q16: What guarantees are in place that your data is fully eradicated should you decide the cloud isn't for you?

My Answer: You've seen the news and countless stories about companies' data being discovered by the public in an unencrypted or non-eradicated state. Just because they delete your data doesn't mean it can't be retrieved. At TOSS C3, we perform a multi-pass data eradication process that exceeds the requirements of the DOD 5220.22-M data eradication standards. Once the process is complete, we send you a certificate of destruction guaranteeing the proper steps have been taken and your data is no longer retrievable by any means.

Q17: How much bandwidth do we need to run everything in the cloud?

My Answer: Our average client with light to moderate printing and scanning uses 256Kbps/user. So if you have 20 users, you will want to have an internet connection capable of 5Mbps/5Mbps. If you print and/or scan in moderate to high volume, you will want twice that amount.

Q18: Where excited about the cloud, yet nervous that we'll be stuck if we don't like it?

My Answer: On average, 10% of the companies we consult with, have this question. We know the cloud will be amazing for you, but you don't, yet. To mitigate the risk, TOSS offers a 90-Day Risk-Free-Guarantee. Here's how it works. Once you've approved the Cloud Conversion Solution, deposits are paid, and your cloud platform is up and running. You will have 90-days to use your cloud system without the risk of being stuck in a long-term agreement, should you decide the cloud is not for you. Simply let us know within the 90-day period that you want to cancel our cloud agreement, and we'll work with your team to put your system back the way it was.

Q19: What IT services are covered under the base cloud agreement?

My Answer:

1. All Microsoft Licensing that's under a Cloud agreement.
2. All support on the Cloud-side for the Microsoft Licensing under Cloud agreement.
3. Hosting of the agreed upon Microsoft and non- Microsoft line of business applications.
4. Patches and same version updates for the Microsoft and non-Microsoft applications.
5. Assistance logging in from an endpoint to your cloud.
6. All access from the internet to your cloud. For example if your cloud access application and system are functional, and the internet is up and running, but you can't reach your cloud.

** TOSS C3 has over 35 cloud products to enhance your cloud experience and ensure both cyber-security and business continuity.*

Q20: Will your system be managed by a certified & compliant cloud provider?

My Answer: In 2011 SAS70 certification was replaced by SSAE16 SOC certification, the new standards for evaluating and reporting on internal controls at service organizations. If you're in the Healthcare industry, then in addition to SSAE16, it is required that your service providers are HIPAA certified as well. TOSS C3 maintains the latest certifications and undergoes annual audits required to provide services to the Financial, Banking, Healthcare, Insurance, Legal, Accounting, and all cross-industry businesses.

Chapter Eight

Contracts, Payment Schedules & Rate Negotiations

Now that you've gone through the work of finding the perfect computer consultant, make sure you don't throw all your hard work down the drain by not securing a clear, concise, win-win contract. It's your best defense against being ripped off and disappointed. It also helps both sides completely understand what is expected, how the work will be done, and your acceptable standards. In some instances, it makes sense to have a qualified attorney review your contracts; however, this chapter will outline some of the basics to include in your contract to make sure you get what you want.

In general, the more detailed the contract is, the better it is for both sides. Don't be afraid of lengthy contracts that spell everything out in specific detail, but DO be cautious of contracts you
don't understand.

Once you've decided on a consultant, ask to meet with him to go over every detail verbally. It's a good idea to prepare for this meeting by outlining your expectations and conditions of satisfaction for the work to be done. The clearer you are on what you want and how you want the work performed, the better your chances are of getting it done right. You should also ask your consultant to bring a copy of his original proposal or quote, as well as a list of deliverables, deadlines, guarantees and other policies and procedures.

This meeting is best done in a face-to-face setting either in person or via video conferencing. You can negotiate your contract over the phone, but our experience shows that greater clarification and detail comes when we meet with our clients.

Warranties, Guarantees and Making Things Right

One of the main things you want to clarify in your contract is exactly what your consultant does and does not guarantee. Make sure you are as specific as possible. For example, if a computer you purchase through your consultant has a hard-drive failure, will he be responsible for getting it replaced with the manufacturer, or will you be? If you experience a problem with the network your consultant recently upgraded or installed, is support included, or charged at an extra rate? Also, if you are unhappy with the work, what happens? Will he redo the job at no extra charge? Will he refund part or all of your money?

Payment Terms

As we mentioned in Chapter 3, a consultant will usually require some type of down payment on a project before he gets started, and payment for any hardware or software purchases up front. However, for non-cloud projects, you should never pay a consultant in full before a project is started. Additionally, you should not be asked to pay the balance of a non-cloud project until it is completed to your satisfaction. As a rule of thumb, try to reserve 20-50% of the total non-cloud project balance to make sure your consultant stays "on the ball" and remains eager to complete your project.

Regardless of what you agree upon, your payment schedule should be detailed in a written contract. This includes exact payment dates, amounts, and specifically what work and conditions of satisfaction have to be met before payment is made. Don't be alarmed if your consultant includes a condition that all work will cease for nonpayment. This is standard and not unreasonable.

Project Timeline and Completion Date

If your project is time-sensitive, you'll want to include not only a definite completion date, but also "slippage" terms that gives you some type of compensation for every day or week over the deadline. Include the phrase that your project is "extremely time-sensitive" and stress the importance of the completion date in writing.

If your project is lengthy, it makes sense to have a project timeline that includes milestones, or the phases that your project will be completed in, and payments tied to the completion of these. This will keep your consultant on track and prevent you from realizing in the 11th hour that your project is way overdue.

Important: Some projects will require your involvement in testing and approving applications and processes designed by your consultant. Make sure you allot time in your busy schedule for testing so you don't delay the project.

Changes, Modifications and "Scope Creep"

Scope creep is a term used by consultants to describe the changes and modifications clients request to a project after the contract has been signed. In some cases, these "tiny" changes result in more work for the consultant and delays in the project's timeline.

For example, let's suppose you decide it's time to upgrade your network. Your consultant provides you with a game plan and a quote for what it will take to upgrade your entire system. However, halfway through the project, you decide that you want to give your traveling sales team secure remote access to the network—something that was not discussed in the original project and proposal. Although it seems to be a simple request, it may take additional hardware, software and hours of work to set up.

Therefore, it's normal and customary for a consultant to outline an hourly rate for all projects, changes and tasks requested by the client *after* the contract has been signed. Just make sure that the hourly rate or amount for any changes is not unreasonable, *and* that it is clearly defined in the contract you sign. In most cases, the consultant will agree to a discounted rate for additional work resulting from changes you make to the original agreement. Again, be sure you have that rate in writing so he doesn't double the rate halfway into your project.

Word of caution: Whenever you request a change to your existing contract or scope of work, make sure you get the change order in writing. If your consultant is a professional, he will require you to sign a written contract addendum; but if he doesn't, make sure you press for one. Don't fall into the trap of verbal "he said, she said" agreements; they will only come back to haunt you. All change orders should include:

- The specific changes to be made
- The date of the request
- A detailed description of the work to be done
- Your conditions of satisfaction
- The additional charges
- Guarantees or warranties
- A new completion date for your project (if necessary)
- This document should be signed by both you and your consultant.

Hardware, Software and Materials

Many computer consultants will gladly research and quote the cost of various hardware and software for the completion of a project. Some will even offer to custom-build your server and workstations instead of purchasing them from a hardware distributor. In most cases, these non-branded computers are every bit as reliable as branded machines offered by Dell, HP or Lenovo. Either way, you want to keep in mind that your consultant is probably not making a lot of money on selling hardware and software and, in many cases, will only resell it to you as a convenience (one-stop shopping).

That's why you want to detail in your contract who is responsible for the warranty on the equipment. If something goes wrong, do you want your consultant to handle it, or will you? Most consultants will charge for handling the warranty repairs on your equipment; don't make the mistake of assuming that, because he sold it to you, he is responsible for manufacturer defects, or that he will do the repairs free. If you expect him to handle this, you must detail that in your contract.

Hours and Conditions of Work

Another point you want to consider before signing on the dotted line is how and when the work will be completed. One of the biggest inconveniences of having a consultant work on your network is the downtime it costs you.

In some situations, it may be necessary for you and all of your employees to log off the network so your consultant may complete certain tasks. If you only need to log off for a short time, it's probably a minor inconvenience; however, if you are upgrading your entire network, or installing a new system, you could be down for several hours.

To prevent your business from being disrupted for long periods, ask your consultant how much downtime the repair or project will require. If you can't afford to be offline for that long, ask that any major upgrades, installations or repairs be done after hours or on weekends. It may cost a bit more, but most consultants will gladly accommodate you if you ask in advance.

Arbitration and Cancellation Clauses

While this book is dedicated to helping you find a great consultant whom you will never want to fire, there still is a chance that you could end up hiring the wrong one. If that happens, you want to make sure your contract is written to protect your rights and keep you from being taken advantage of. Again, this section should not be considered legal advice, and should not take the place of a qualified attorney reviewing your contact. However, for the sake of completeness, we will touch on what you need to protect yourself in the event that your consultant doesn't fulfill his promises.

First, consider adding an arbitration clause in your contract. Arbitration is often a faster, easier and less-expensive way to resolve a dispute between you and the consultant you hired. Some consultants will specify an arbitration company in their contract. If you don't like their choice, make sure you voice your concern and recommend an alternative independent arbitration company.

Next, make sure your contract has a clear cancellation policy. If you discover that you hired the wrong consultant and want out of your contract, you'll want a written clause that details not only how to cancel the contract, but also what you will owe. Determining whether you are entitled to a refund, or are required to pay for work completed, will often have to be negotiated by the arbitration company you designate in your contract.

Quick Tip: If you decide you need to cancel a contract, make sure you send your cancellation notice by certified mail, return receipt requested. This will give you proof that your consultant has received your cancellation notice.

The biggest "secret" to securing a win-win contract is to make sure there are no loopholes. Include everything you can think of in writing, no matter how small or insignificant it may seem at the moment.

And finally, you should always have a qualified legal counsel review your agreement, especially if it involves a lengthy and expensive project. The little bit of money you will invest in a good attorney will go a long way to ensure a happy, hassle-free project!

Chapter Nine

Technical Terms Explained in Plain English

ASP: *Application Service Provider*, a third-party company that manages and distributes software-based services and solutions to their customers over a wide-area network, usually the Internet.

Blackberry Enterprise Server (BES): A software and service that connects to collaboration software (Microsoft Exchange, Lotus Domino, Novell GroupWise) on enterprise networks and redirects emails and synchronizes contacts and calendaring information between servers, workstations and BlackBerry mobile devices.

Cloud Computing: Internet based computing, whereby shared resources, software, and information are provided to computers and other devices on demand, as with the electricity grid.

Content Filtering: Software that prevents users from accessing or sending objectionable content via your network. Although this usually refers to Web content, many programs also screen inbound and outbound e-mails for offensive and confidential information. This software is not designed for virus, worm or hacker prevention.

CPU: *Central Processing Unit*, the brains of a computer.

DHCP: *Dynamic Host Configuration Protocol*, a method for dynamically assigning IP addresses to devices on request, rather than explicitly programming an IP address into each device. If you have a server on your network, configuring that server as a DHCP server will make it much easier to add or reconfigure individual workstations on the network.

Default Gateway: In a TCP/IP network, this is the gateway that computers on that network use to send data to, and receive it from, computers and networks outside of the local network. Typically, this is the router or firewall that connects the local network to the public Internet, although it might also be a router that connects to another remote server or computer within the same company.

DMZ: ***Demilitarized Zone***, a separate area of your network that is isolated from both the Internet and your protected internal network. A DMZ is usually created by your firewall to provide a location for devices such as Web servers that you want to be accessible from the public Internet.

DNS: ***Domain Name System*** (or ***Server***), an Internet service that translates domain names into IP addresses. Even though most domain names are alphabetic, hardware devices (like your PC) can only send data to a specific IP address. When you type www.microsoft.com into your Web browser, or send an e-mail message to someone@business.com, your Web browser and e-mail server have to be able to look up the IP address that corresponds to the microsoft.com Web server, or to the mail server that receives e-mail for business.com. DNS is the mechanism for doing this lookup.

DSL: ***Digital Subscriber Line***, a high-speed Internet service delivered over a telephone line.

Firewall: A device or software program designed to protect your network from unauthorized access over the Internet. It may also provide Network Address Translation (NAT) and Virtual Private Network (VPN) functionality.

Fractional T-1: One or more channels of a T-1 service. A complete T-1 carrier contains 24 channels, each of which provides 64 Kbps. Most phone companies also sell fractional T-1 lines, which provide less bandwidth but are less expensive. See T-1.

Hosted Applications (i.e. Hosted SharePoint or Hosted Exchange): A service whereby a provider makes a software (i.e.

email) and space available on a server so its clients can host their data on that server.

IP Address: An identifier for a computer or device on a TCP/IP network. The format for an IP address is a 32-bit numeric address separated by periods (example: 207.46.20.60). Within an isolated network, you can assign an IP address at random, as long as each IP address on that network is unique. However, if you are connecting a network or computer to the Internet, you must have a registered IP address (also called an Internet address) to avoid duplicates.

POP3: *Post Office Protocol 3,* a method of communication between an e-mail server and an e-mail client. In most cases, when the client software connects to a POP3 server, the e-mail messages are downloaded to the client and are no longer available on the server.

Protocol: An agreed format for transmitting data between two devices.

T-1: A dedicated digital transmission line that sends and receives data at a rate of 1.544 Mbps. T-1 lines can be used to carry voice traffic, data traffic or a combination of both.

TCP/IP: *Transmission Control Protocol/Internet Protocol,* the basic language that governs traffic on the global Internet, as well as on most private networks.

URL: *Uniform Resource Locator,* the global address of documents, Websites and other resources on the Web.

VoIP: *Voice-Over-IP,* a category of hardware and software that allows you to use the Internet to make phone calls and send faxes. This technology is becoming very popular with businesses and home users alike because it greatly reduces telephone costs.

VPN: *Virtual Private Network,* a network constructed by using public wires (the Internet) to connect nodes (usually computers and servers). A VPN uses encryption and other security mechanisms to ensure that only authorized users can access the network and the data it holds. This allows businesses to connect to other servers and computers located in remote offices, from home, or while traveling.

An Invitation to the Reader

The reason I published this book was to fortify business owners with the basic knowledge they need to make a great decision when choosing a computer consultant. I believe a qualified computer consultant can contribute to your business success just like a great marketing consultant, attorney, accountant or financial advisor.

The technology industry is so new, and growing at such a rapid pace, that most business owners can't keep up with all the latest whiz-bang gadgets, alphabet soup acronyms, and choices available to them. Plus, many of the "latest and greatest" technological developments have a shelf life of six months before they become obsolete or completely out-of-date. Sorting through this rapidly-moving mess of information to formulate an intelligent plan for growing a business requires a professional who not only understands technology and how it works, but also understands how people and businesses need to work with technology for progress.

Unfortunately, the complexity of technology makes it easy for a business owner to fall victim to an incompetent or dishonest computer consultant. When this happens, it creates feelings of mistrust toward all technology consultants and vendors, which makes it difficult for those of us striving to deliver exceptional value and service to our clients.

Therefore, my purpose is to not only give you the information you need to find an honest, competent computer consultant, but in doing so, to raise the standards and quality of services for all consultants in my industry. I believe that, the more this topic is discussed, the better it will become for all involved.

I certainly want your feedback on the ideas in this book. If you try the strategies I've outlined and they work, please send me your story. If you've had a bad experience with a computer consultant, I want to hear those horror stories as well. If you have additional tips and insights that we haven't considered, please share them with me. I might even use them in a future book!

Again, the more aware you are of what it takes to find and hire great consultants in every aspect of your business—not just technology—the stronger your business will become. I am truly passionate about building an organization that delivers uncommon service to my clients. I want to help business executives see the true competitive advantages technology can deliver to your business, and not just view it as an expensive necessity and source of problems.

Your contributions, thoughts and stories pertaining to my goal will make it possible. Please write, call or e-mail me with your ideas.

VALUABLE HASSLE-FREE COMPUTER SUPPORT COUPON FOR FREE 27-POINT PROBLEM PREVENTION NETWORK AUDIT

($995 Value)

Don't let computer problems take over your business! If you are a business owner with eight or more PCs, I'd like to offer you a FREE 27-Point Problem Prevention Network Audit to:

- Diagnose any ongoing problems or concerns you have with the computers on your network.
- Scan for hidden viruses, spyware and loopholes in your network security that could allow hackers and other cybercriminals to access your confidential information.
- Check your system backups to make sure they are not corrupted and can be recovered in case of an emergency.
- Review your network configuration and peripheral devices to ensure that you are getting the maximum performance and speed from your machines.
- Review your server file logs to look for looming problems or conflicts that can cause unexpected downtime.
- Check that all security updates and patches are in place.

HASSLE-FREE COMPUTER SUPPORT
COUPON ($995 Value)

Call Greg Hanna at +1.888.884.TOSS and just say that you want the FREE 27-Point Problem Prevention Network Audit

No duplicate coupons or copies will be accepted.
This offer can't be sold, traded or combined with any other offers

BOOK ORDER FORM

If you enjoyed this book, share it with others! Use this form to order extra copies for friends, colleagues, clients or members of your association. Please allow 2-4 weeks for delivery.

Quantity Discounts:

1-9 copies = $19.95, 10-49 copies = $16.95 each
50-99 copies = $13.95 each
100 or more copies = Call for discounts and wholesale prices

Information:

Name: ____

Company: ____

Address: ____

City: ____

State/Province: _______________________________________

ZIP/Postal Code: ______________________________________

Of copies __________ @ $__________ Total: $_________________

Add shipping and handling @ $3 per book: $____________________

To Order by Mail:

Please make check or money order payable to:
TOSS Corporation
153 Northboro Rd., Ste. 21, Southborough, MA 01772

To Order by Fax: Complete/Sign/Fax form to **+1.508.820.2991**

Credit Card: ❑ Visa ❑ MC ❑ Amex ❑ Discover
Card Number: ____
Expiration Date: _______________________________________
Signature: ____

Thank you for your order